× 200 ×

JAPANESE CROSS STITCH DESIGNS

Traditional, geometric, retro and floral patterns for mindful stitching

Saeko Endo

DAVID & CHARLES
—PUBLISHING—

www.davidandcharles.com

Contents

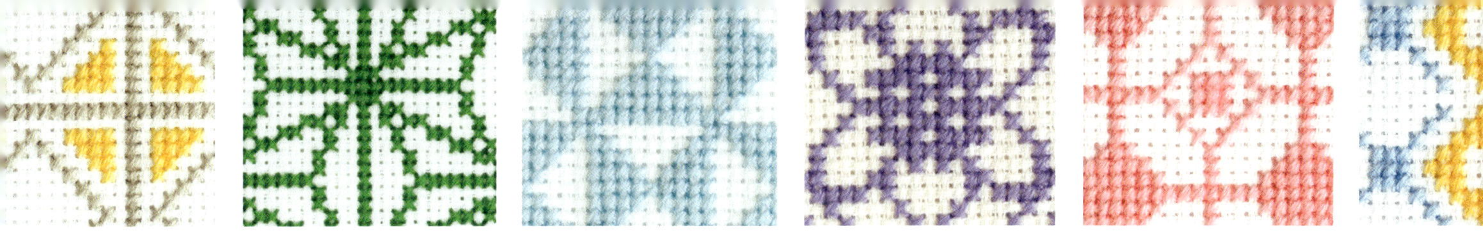

Introduction

If you look around, you'll find that we are surrounded by patterns—they exist in nature, from the spots and stripes of animal markings, to the waves of the ocean, to the fractals of a snowflake. Over the years, I myself have become a student of pattern through my embroidery work.

I often draw inspiration from the past, studying design books by artists such as Tomizo Yorozu, who saw patterns as something that would enrich everyday life and devised the idea of using them in handicrafts and products that people can enjoy.

I've also studied the patterns that have appeared on kimonos since ancient times. Historically, kimonos have featured a wide variety of patterns including classic designs, auspicious designs that are considered to be lucky, designs with plant and animal motifs and geometric designs. Some of the designs in this book are attempts to recreate *ise katagami*, which is the Japanese craft of carving paper stencils for dyeing textiles.

Throughout the book, I've explored the concepts of orientation and repeat, creating continuous patterns that can spread out in all directions, as well as designs intended to be used as borders or centre motifs. I've also experimented with colour to illustrate how the same motif can have a completely different look and feel based on colour scheme.

In fact, my favourite thing about patterns is the infinite number of possibilities that are out there. My hope is that this book will introduce you to the fun and excitement of creating patterns stitched in embroidery thread.

—*Saeko Endo*

Cross Stitch Basics

Before you start stitching, let's cover a few basic techniques. Learning these fundamentals will help you understand how to stitch the cross stitch designs included in this book and create fun and interesting patterns.

TOOLS & MATERIALS

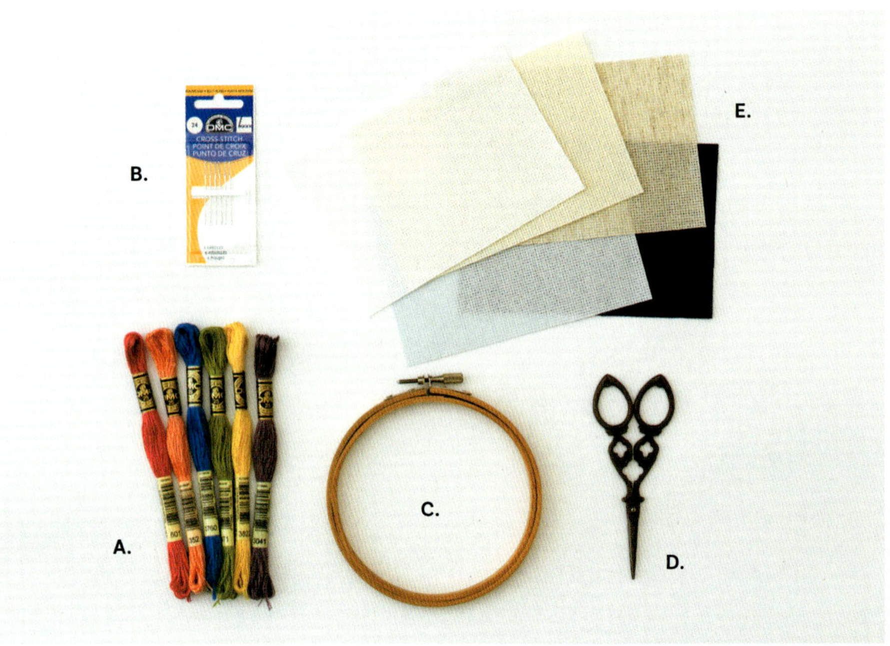

A. Embroidery Floss

There are many different types of embroidery floss available today. You'll find floss made from different materials, such as cotton, silk, linen and wool. Each type of embroidery floss offers unique characteristics and possesses different weights and textures. All of the designs in this book were stitched with DMC No. 25 embroidery floss. This 100% cotton thread is composed of six strands that can be separated. Use two strands of floss, unless otherwise noted.

B. Needles

Use needles with a rounded tip designed specifically for cross stitching. The rounded tip prevents the needle from getting caught between the woven threads of the fabric. Choose a needle size that corresponds with the number of strands of floss and the count of the embroidery fabric so that the holes in the fabric will not be noticeable after stitching. Remember, the larger the number, the thinner the needle and the smaller the eye. DMC size 24 cross stitch needles were used to stitch the designs in this book.

C. Embroidery hoop

Insert the fabric into a hoop before stitching. The hoop will stretch the fabric taut and make it easier to stitch. Hoops are available in various sizes, so choose one that will fit the specific design being stitched.

D. Scissors

Look for a pair of scissors with thin blades to trim threads.

E. Fabric

Unlike other types of embroidery, cross stitching does not require you to transfer the design onto the fabric. Instead, you need to count the number of stitches. As a result, it's best to use fabric designed specifically for cross stitch.

One of these types of fabric is called Aida, which is a 100% cotton evenweave fabric that features a grid-like pattern of holes perfect for stitching. Aida is available in different fabric counts. A fabric's count is the number of holes per inch, which determines the number of stitches per inch. The higher the fabric count, the smaller the finished design will be when it is stitched. All of the designs in this book were stitched on 16 count Aida fabric.

GETTING STARTED

Prepare the Thread

1 Locate one of the ends of the embroidery floss sticking out of the skein. With the label still attached, slowly pull the end of the floss out from the skein and cut a 50cm (20in) long piece.

2 Separate the individual strands of floss one at a time, then realign the desired number of strands. Separating the strands will give the thread more body and prevent knotting while stitching.

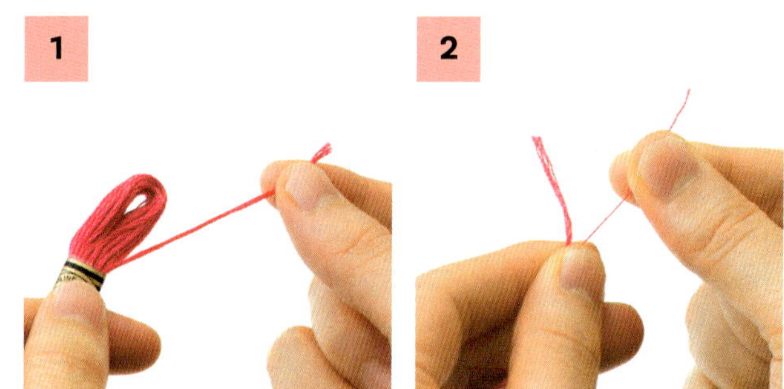

Thread the Needle

1 Fold your thread a short distance away from the end. Next, insert the end of the needle between the two layers of the fold. Press the needle against the fold to create a crease in the thread.

2 Pass the folded end through the eye of needle.

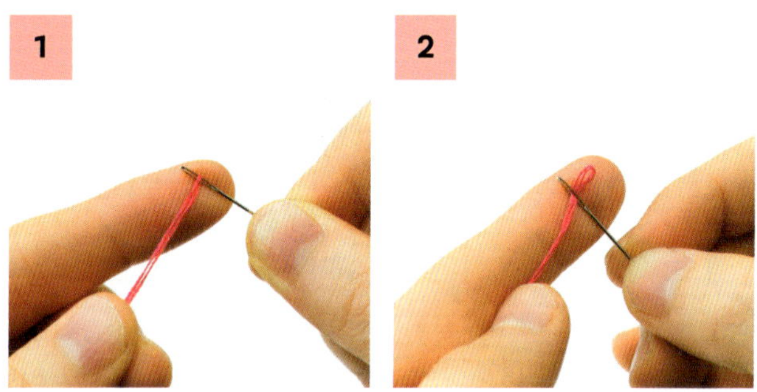

CHANGE THE NUMBER OF STRANDS TO CREATE DIFFERENT FINISHES

The designs in this book were stitched using two strands of DMC No. 25 embroidery floss; however, you can experiment with the number of strands used to create different impressions. The photos to the right show the difference between using one and two strands of floss to stitch the same design. It's also worth noting that even if the same number of strands are used, the finished appearance of the design will change if the fabric count is different. Find your favourite combination of floss strands and fabric count based on the individual design.

HOW TO CROSS STITCH

When Working Horizontally

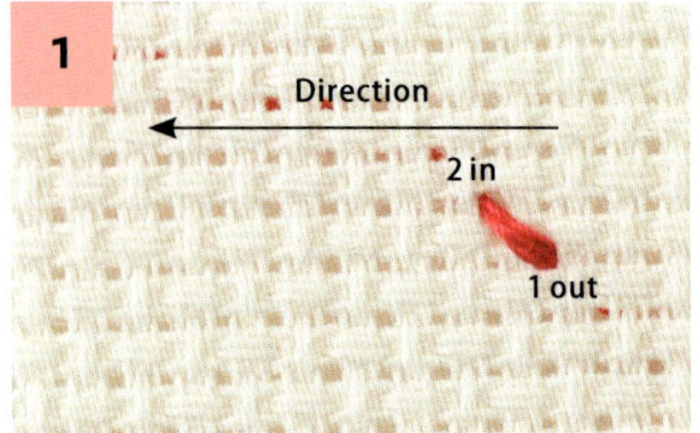

Draw needle out at 1 and insert it back into the fabric at 2.

2

Follow the same process to make stitches to the left of the first stitch, always working in the same direction.

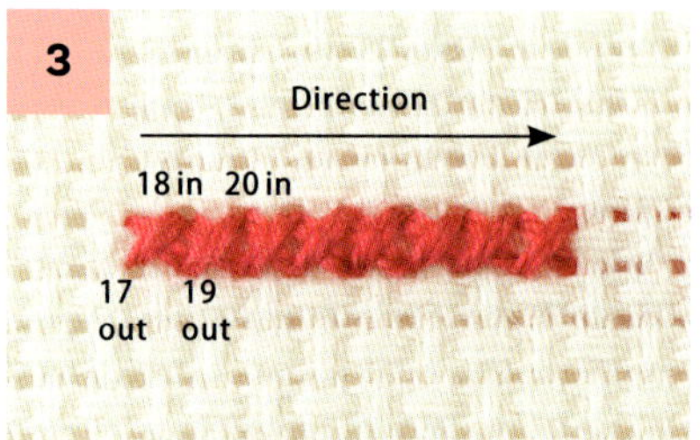

When you reach the end of the row, reverse direction and make stitches on top of those from step 2 in order to complete each X.

Note: Make sure to always cross your stitches in the same direction throughout the entire piece. In this book, the stitches always cross with the / leg on top, but it is fine if the \ leg is on top instead. Just make sure to be consistent!

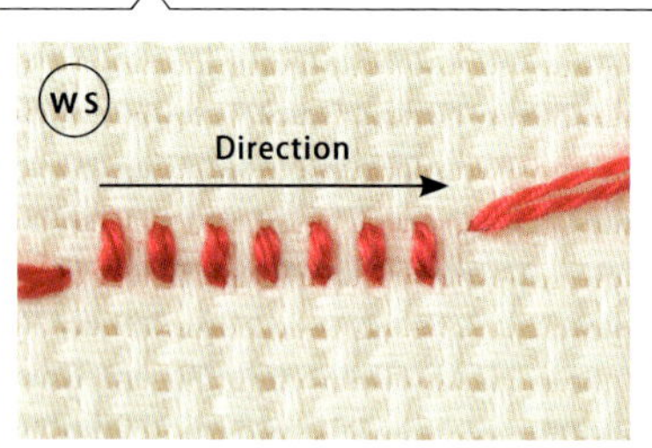

Note: The beginning thread tail has not been finished in order to make it easier to see the movement of the thread.

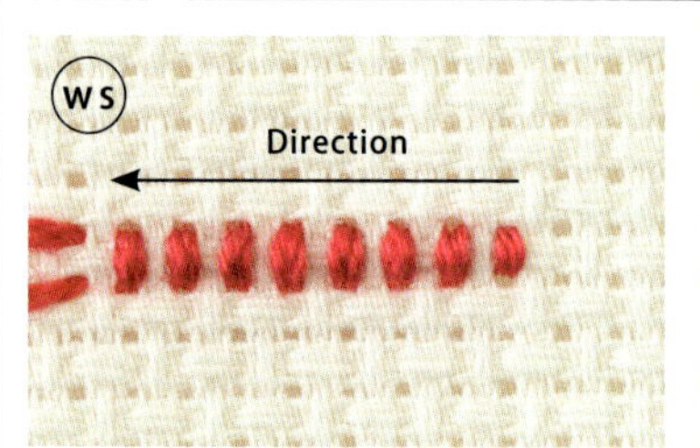

Note: The beginning thread tail has not been finished in order to make it easier to see the movement of the thread.

When Working Vertically

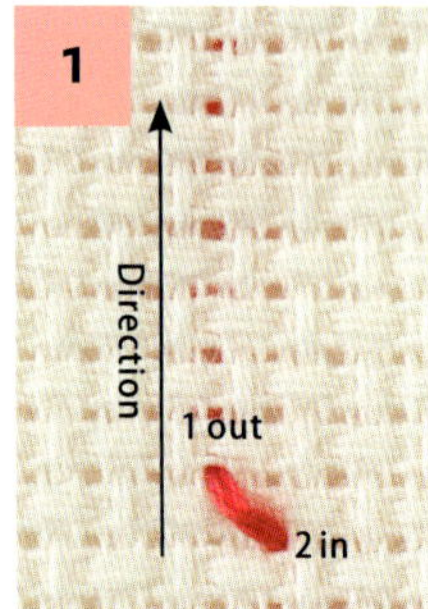

Unlike when working horizontally, you'll make each stitch one X at a time when working vertically. Draw needle out at 1 and insert it back into the fabric at 2.

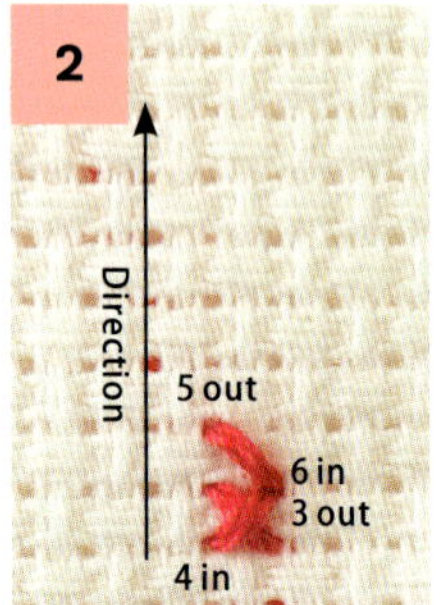

Draw needle out at 3 and insert it back into the fabric at 4 to complete the X. Move up to the next row and draw needle out at 5 and insert it back into the fabric at 6. **Note:** 6 is the same hole as 3.

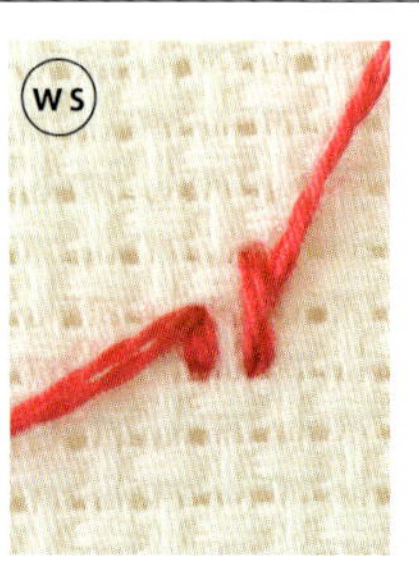

Note: The beginning thread tail has not been finished in order to make it easier to see the movement of the thread.

Continue stitching one X at a time, working from bottom to top.

Note: The beginning thread tail has not been finished in order to make it easier to see the movement of the thread.

OTHER EMBROIDERY STITCHES

Straight Stitch

Draw the needle out at 1 and insert it back into the fabric at 2.

French Knot (wrap twice)

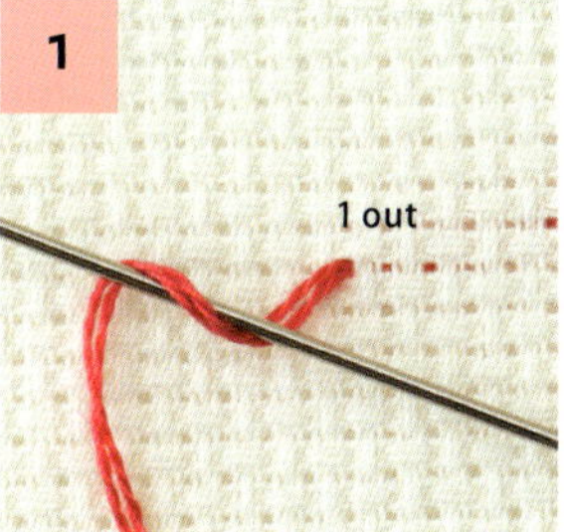

Draw needle out at 1. Wrap thread around the needle twice.
Note: You can wrap the thread around the needle as many times as you'd like. The more wraps, the larger the finished knot.

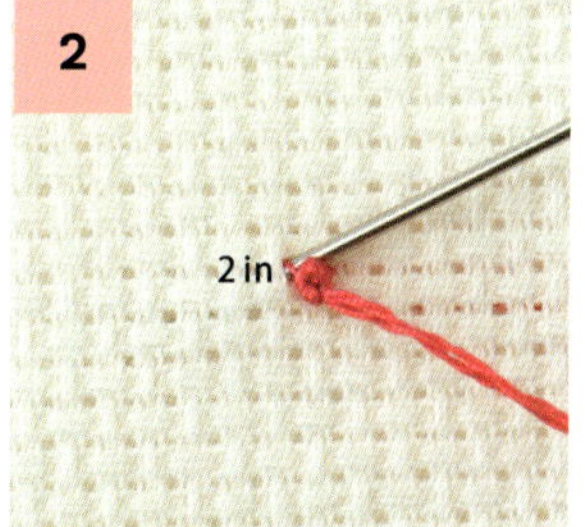

Insert needle back through fabric next to where thread was drawn out. Be careful not to pull the thread too hard or insert it into the same hole as 1 as this may cause the knot to slip through to the wrong side of fabric.

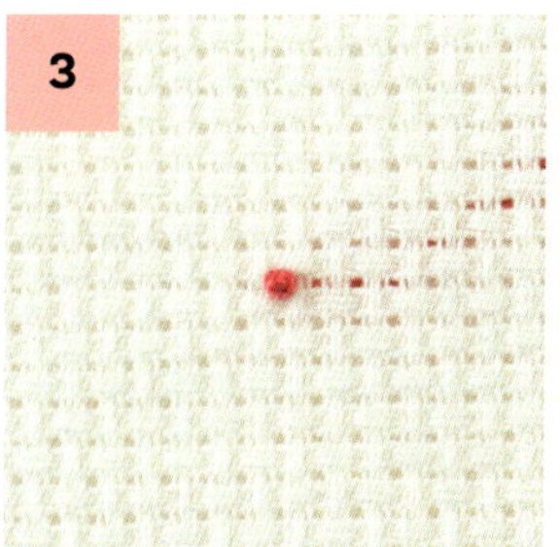

The French knot is complete.

HOW TO START & FINISH

How to Start

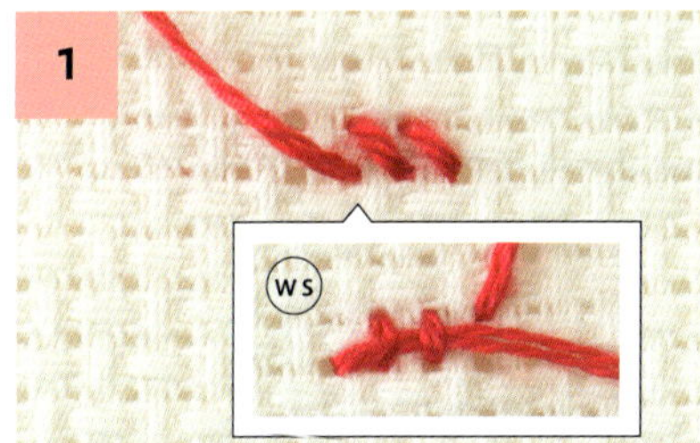

Do not tie a knot at the end of the thread. Instead, start stitching, leaving a 2–3cm (¾–1¼in) thread tail on the wrong side of the work. As you make your first few stitches, stitch over the thread tail on the wrong side of the work so it gets secured in place.

It helps to hold the thread tail in a horizontal line so that your stitches form on top.

Make sure the thread tail is secured under at least three stitches on the wrong side of the work.

How to Finish

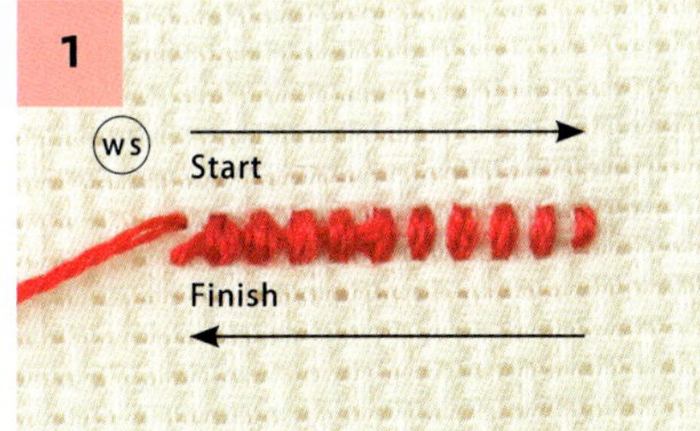

View of the wrong side of the work after stitching. **Note:** The photo above shows the starting thread tail that has been secured.

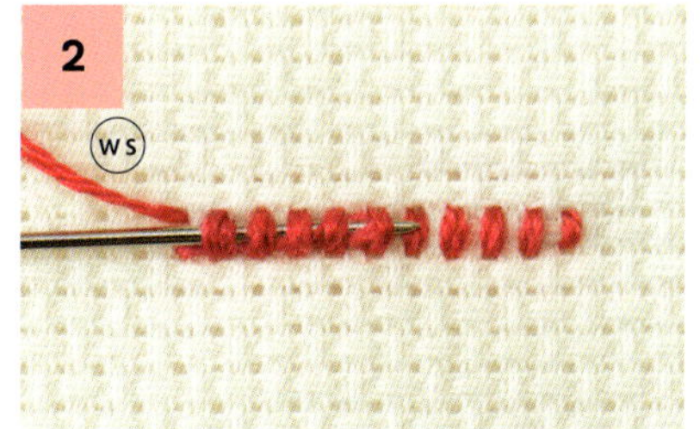

To secure the thread when you are finished stitching, pass the needle under 5–6 stitches on the wrong side of the work.

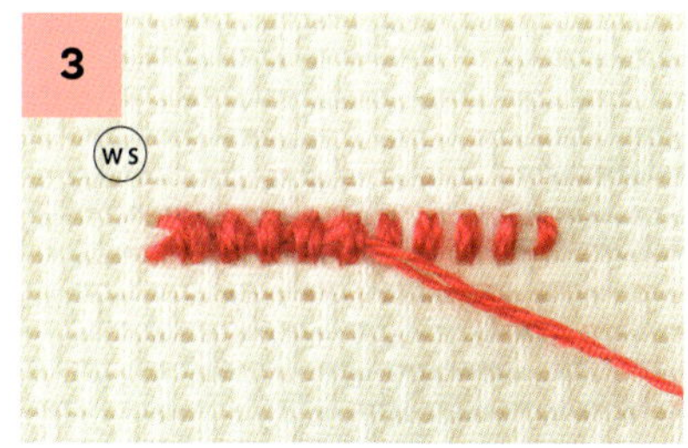

Pull the thread through and trim the excess.

PART ONE

Geometric Patterns

This fun and colourful collection of patterns includes designs inspired by geometric shapes. You'll find motifs featuring stars, circles, hearts, crosses, pinwheels and more!

01 Instructions > page 16

02 Instructions > page 16

03 Instructions > page 16

04 Instructions > page 16

05 Instructions > page 16

06 Instructions > page 16

07 Instructions > page 17

08 Instructions > page 17

09 Instructions > page 17

10 Instructions > page 17

11 Instructions > page 18

12 Instructions > page 19

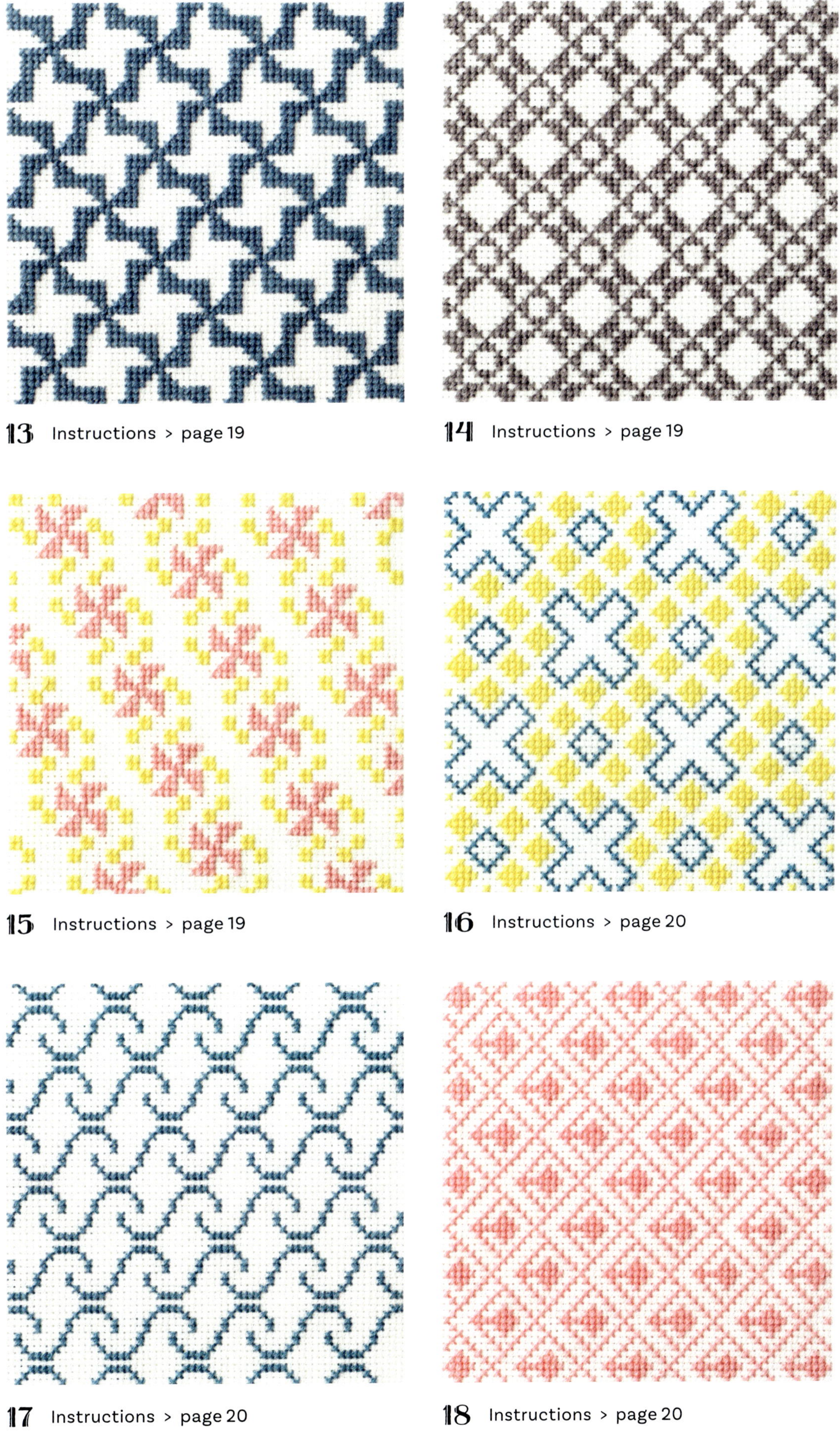

13 Instructions > page 19

14 Instructions > page 19

15 Instructions > page 19

16 Instructions > page 20

17 Instructions > page 20

18 Instructions > page 20

19 Instructions > page 20

20 Instructions > page 20

21 Instructions > page 20

22 Instructions > page 21

23 Instructions > page 21

24 Instructions > page 21

25 Instructions > page 21

26 Instructions > page 21

27 Instructions > page 21

28 Instructions > page 22

29 Instructions > page 22

30 Instructions > page 22

31 Instructions > page 22

32 Instructions > page 23

33 Instructions > page 23

34 Instructions > page 23

35 Instructions > page 23

36 Instructions > page 23

01 Photo > *Page 8*

DMC Embroidery Floss ■ 3354

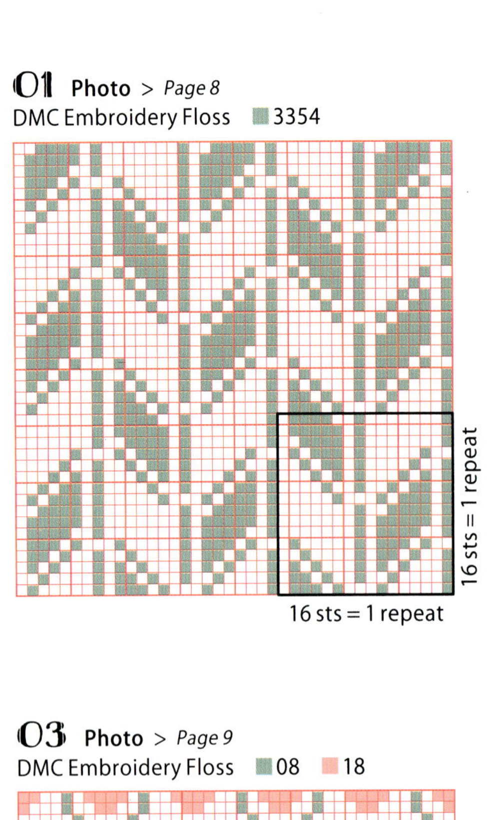

02 Photo > *Page 8*

DMC Embroidery Floss ■ 3354 ■ 18

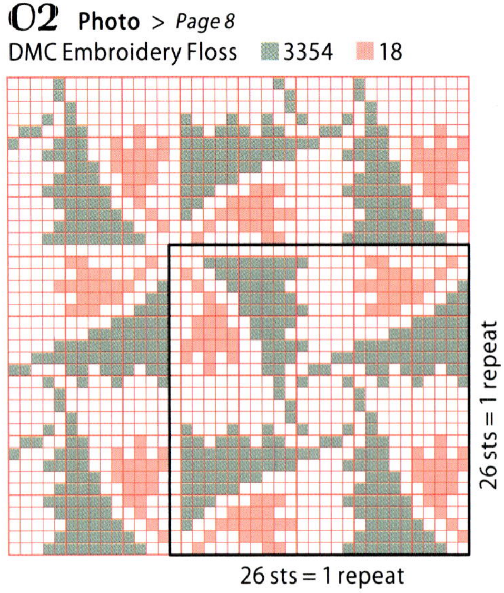

03 Photo > *Page 9*

DMC Embroidery Floss ■ 08 ■ 18

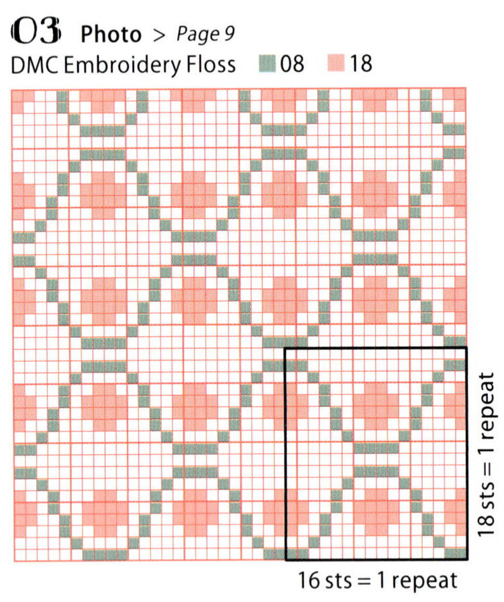

04 Photo > *Page 9*

DMC Embroidery Floss ■ 3354

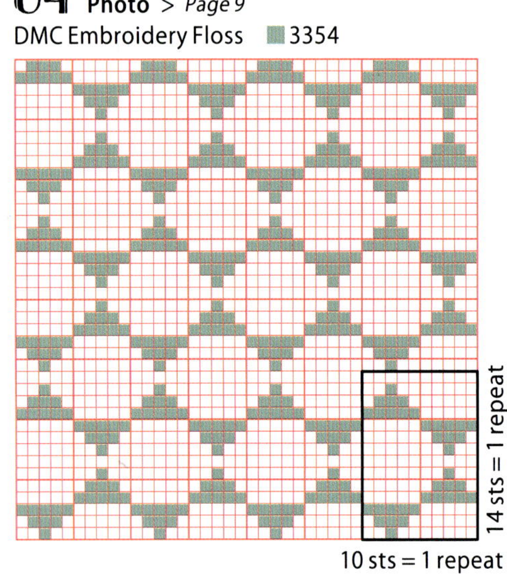

05 Photo > *Page 9*

DMC Embroidery Floss ■ 08

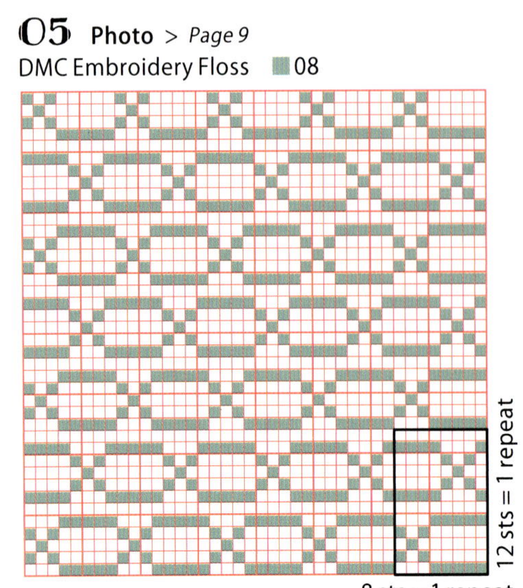

06 Photo > *Page 9*

DMC Embroidery Floss ■ 3354

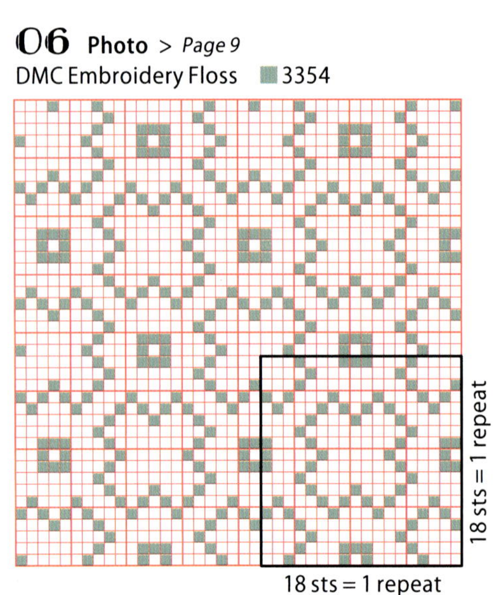

07 Photo > *Page 10*

DMC Embroidery Floss ■ 04 ■ 17

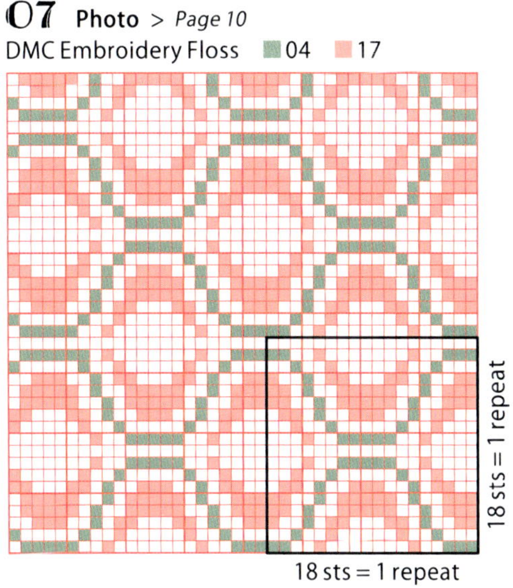

08 Photo > *Page 10*

DMC Embroidery Floss ■ 3354

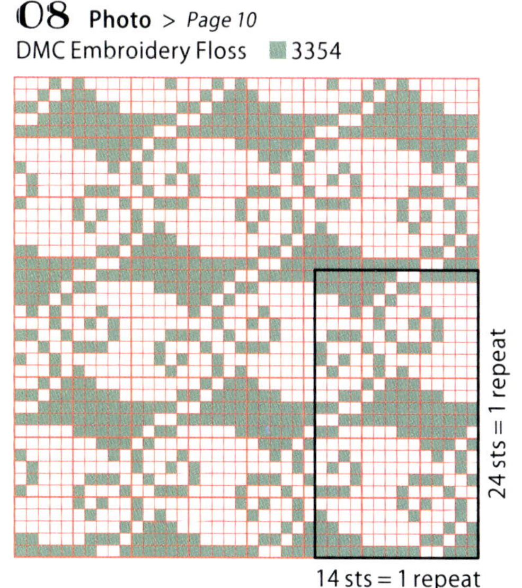

09 Photo > *Page 10*

DMC Embroidery Floss ■ 3810

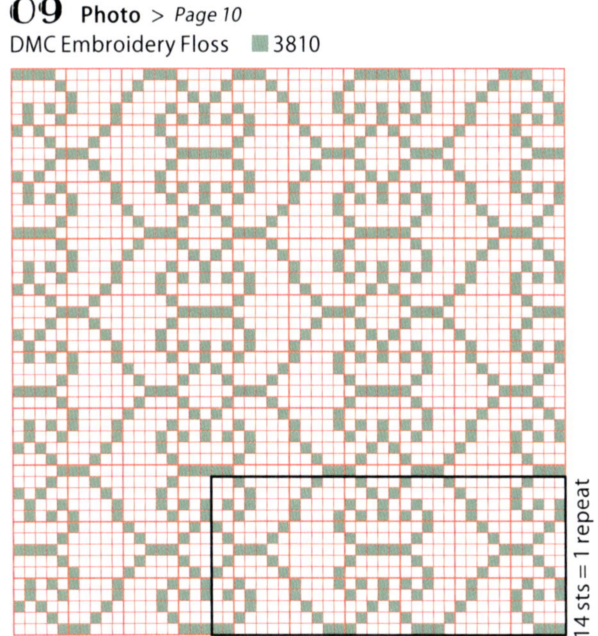

10 Photo > *Page 10*

DMC Embroidery Floss ■ 3354

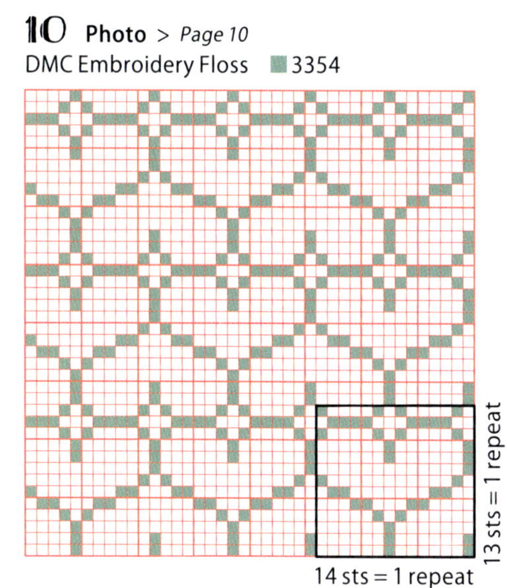

11 **Photo** > *Page 10*

DMC Embroidery Floss ■ 04

12 Photo > *Page 10*

DMC Embroidery Floss ■ 04 ■ 17

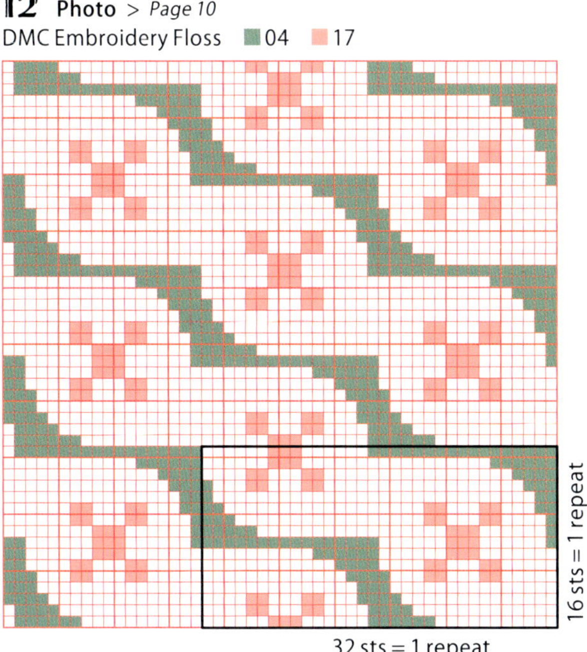

13 Photo > *Page 11*

DMC Embroidery Floss ■ 3810

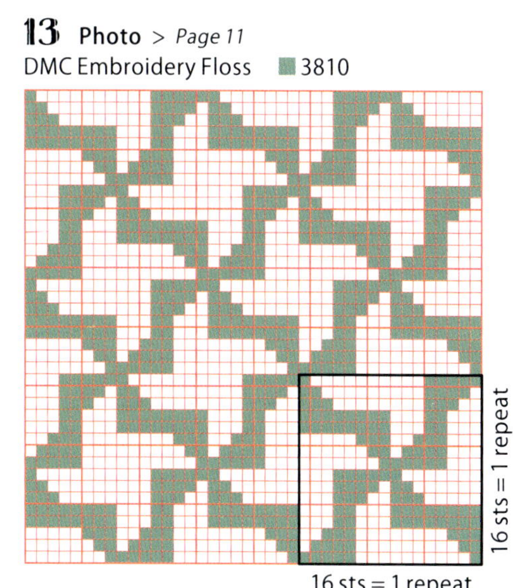

14 Photo > *Page 11*

DMC Embroidery Floss ■ 04

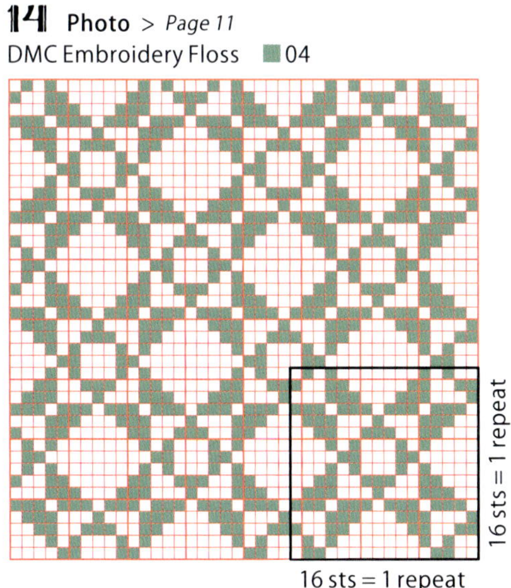

15 Photo > *Page 11*

DMC Embroidery Floss ■ 3354 ■ 17

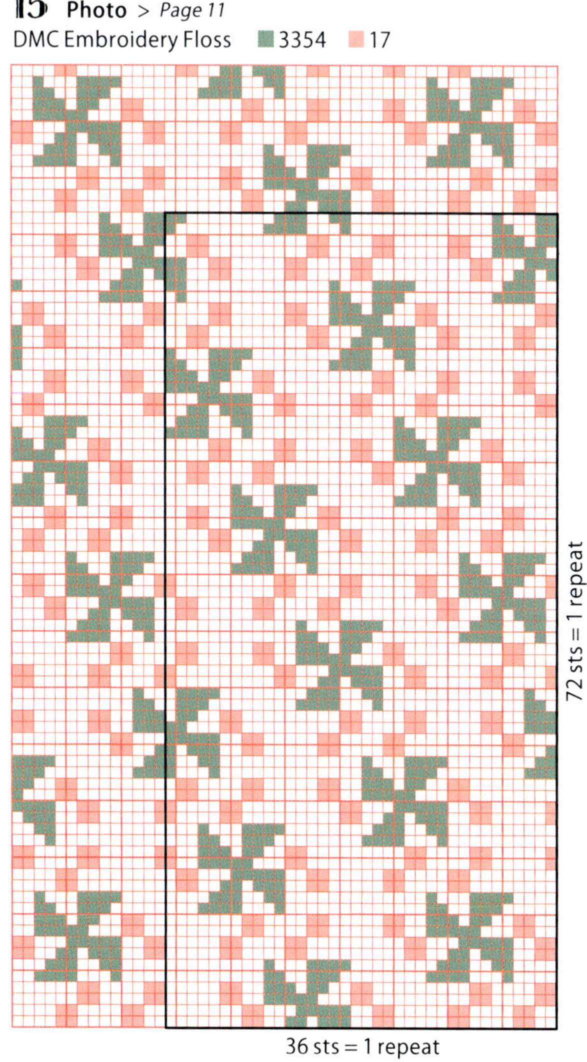

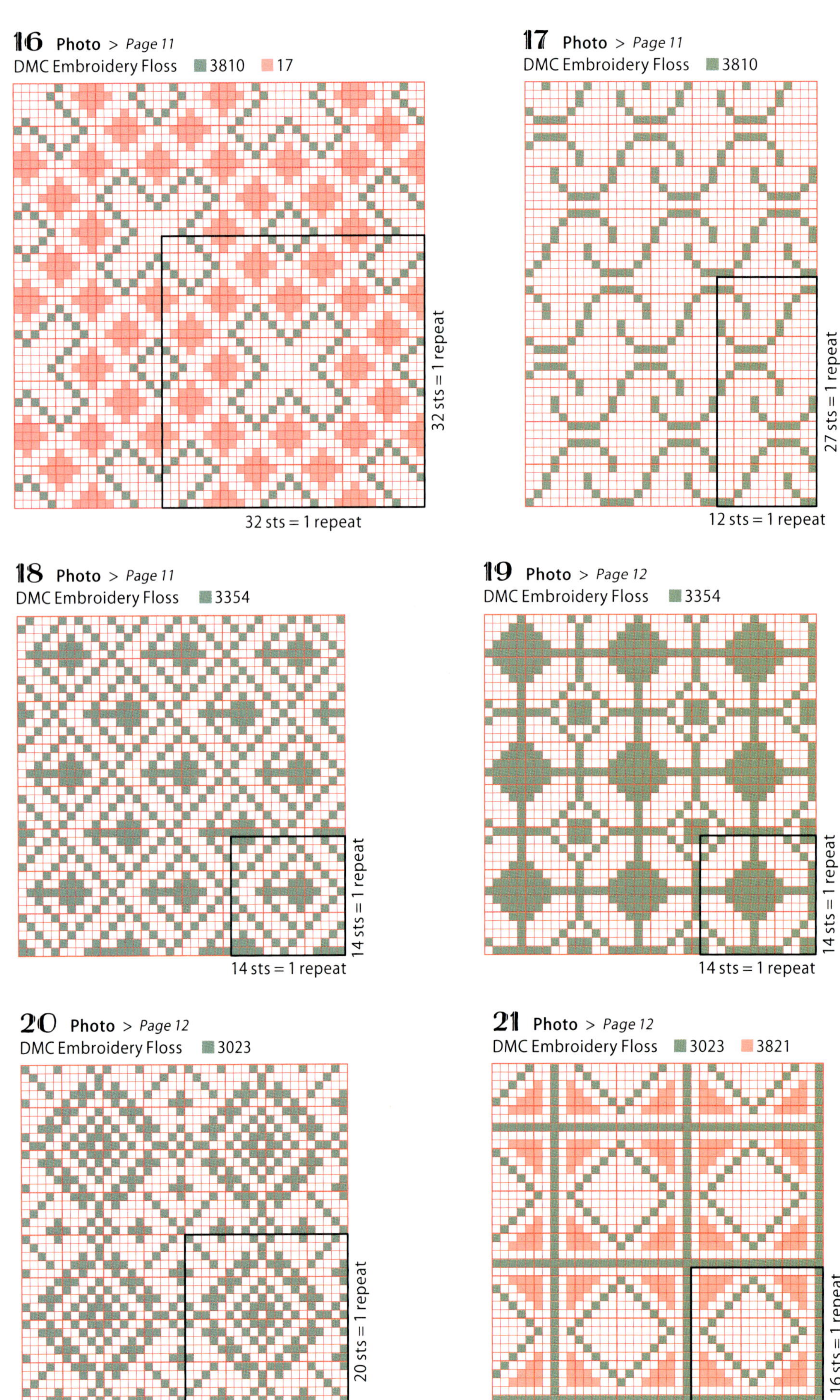
16 Photo > Page 11
DMC Embroidery Floss 3810 17
32 sts = 1 repeat
32 sts = 1 repeat
17 Photo > Page 11
DMC Embroidery Floss 3810
27 sts = 1 repeat
12 sts = 1 repeat
18 Photo > Page 11
DMC Embroidery Floss 3354
14 sts = 1 repeat
14 sts = 1 repeat
19 Photo > Page 12
DMC Embroidery Floss 3354
14 sts = 1 repeat
14 sts = 1 repeat
20 Photo > Page 12
DMC Embroidery Floss 3023
20 sts = 1 repeat
20 sts = 1 repeat
21 Photo > Page 12
DMC Embroidery Floss 3023 3821
16 sts = 1 repeat
16 sts = 1 repeat

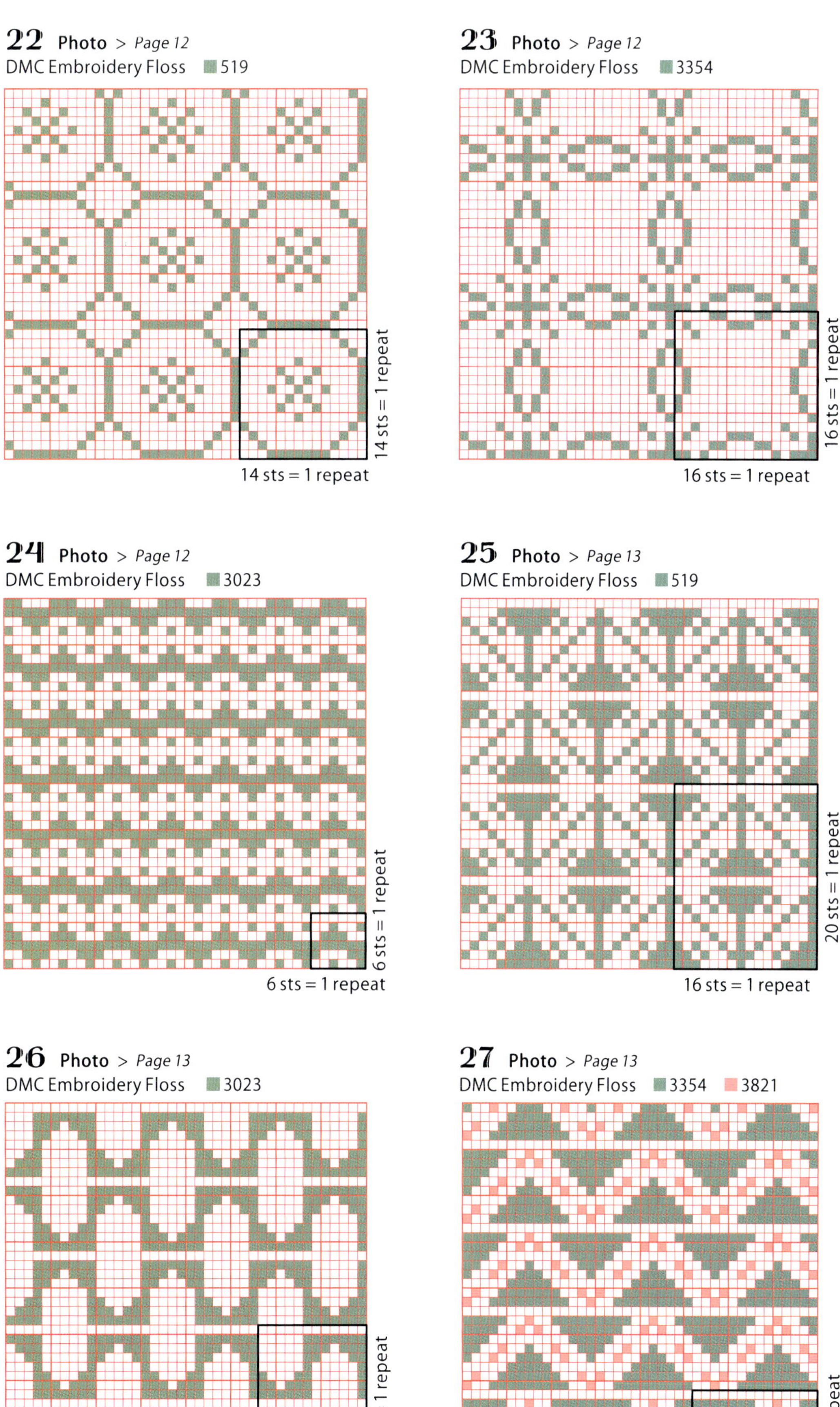
22 Photo > Page 12
DMC Embroidery Floss 519
14 sts = 1 repeat
14 sts = 1 repeat
23 Photo > Page 12
DMC Embroidery Floss 3354
16 sts = 1 repeat
16 sts = 1 repeat
24 Photo > Page 12
DMC Embroidery Floss 3023
6 sts = 1 repeat
6 sts = 1 repeat
25 Photo > Page 13
DMC Embroidery Floss 519
20 sts = 1 repeat
16 sts = 1 repeat
26 Photo > Page 13
DMC Embroidery Floss 3023
16 sts = 1 repeat
12 sts = 1 repeat
27 Photo > Page 13
DMC Embroidery Floss 3354 3821
9 sts = 1 repeat
14 sts = 1 repeat

28 **Photo** > *Page 13*

DMC Embroidery Floss 519 3821

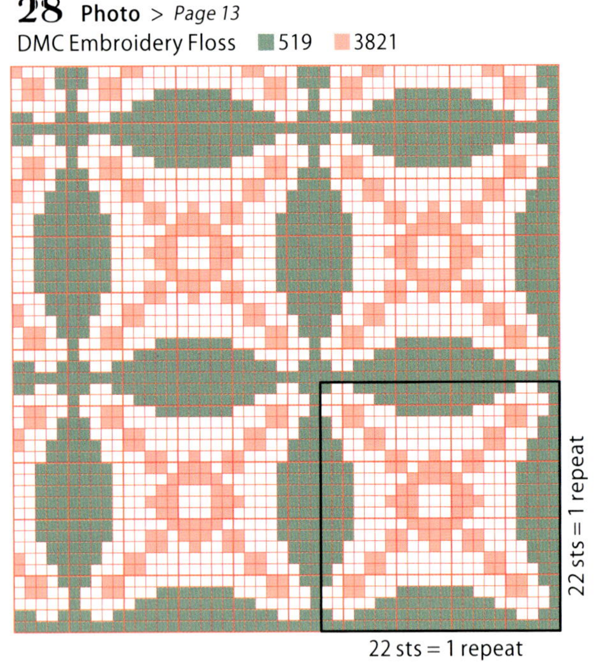

29 **Photo** > *Page 13*

DMC Embroidery Floss 519 3821

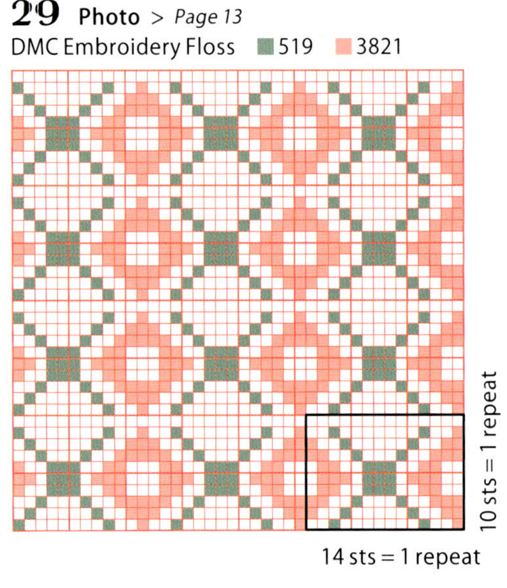

30 **Photo** > *Page 13*

DMC Embroidery Floss 3354

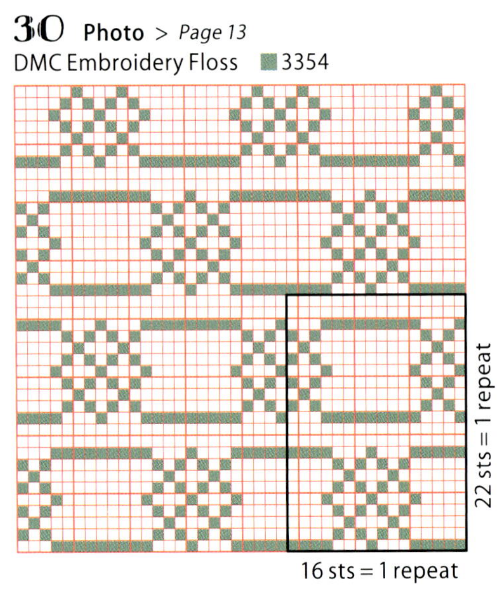

31 **Photo** > *Page 14*

DMC Embroidery Floss 312 18

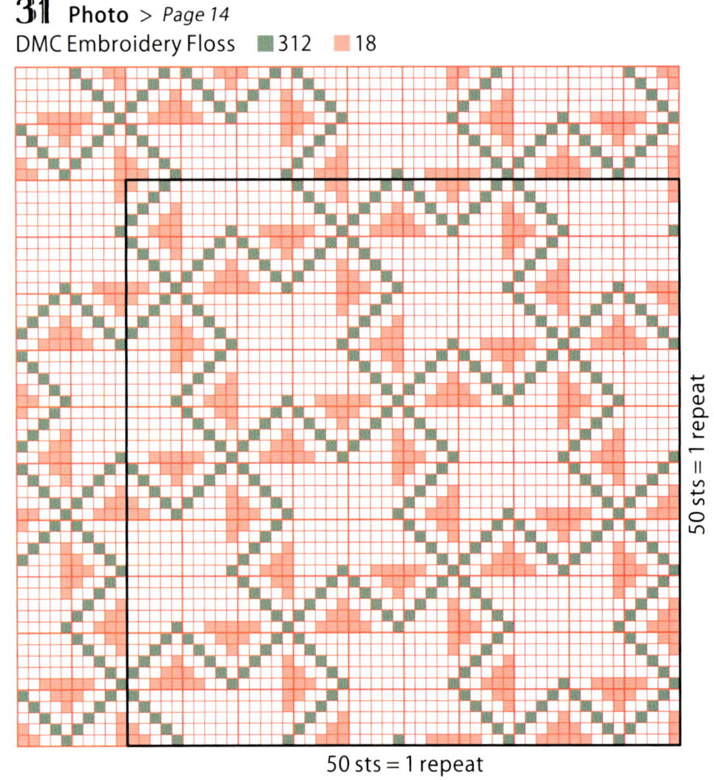

32 Photo > *Page 14*

DMC Embroidery Floss ■ 312

33 Photo > *Page 15*

DMC Embroidery Floss ■ 08

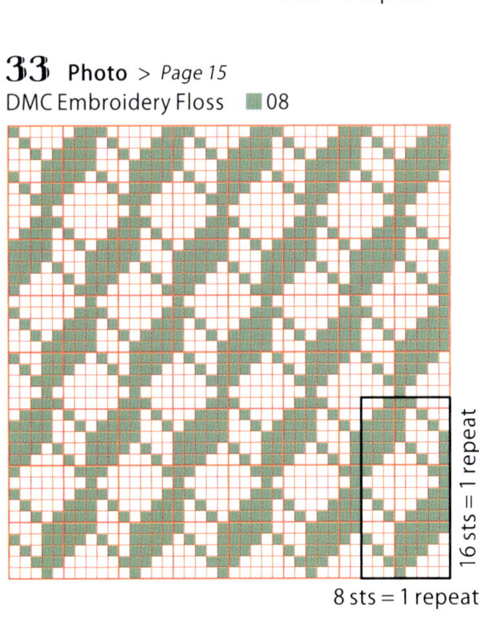

36 Photo > *Page 15*

DMC Embroidery Floss ■ 08 ■ 18

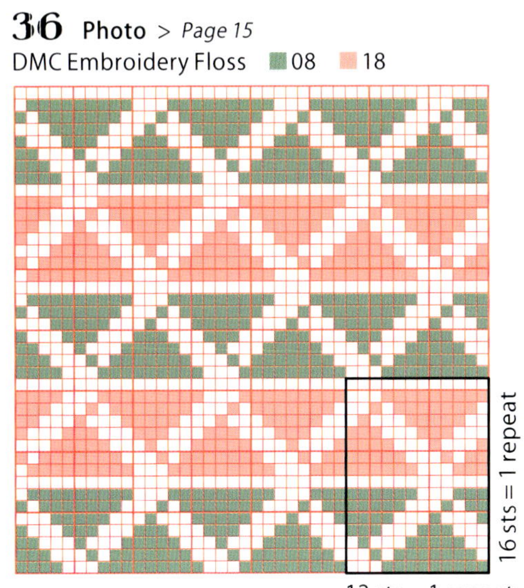

34 Photo > *Page 15*

DMC Embroidery Floss ■ 312

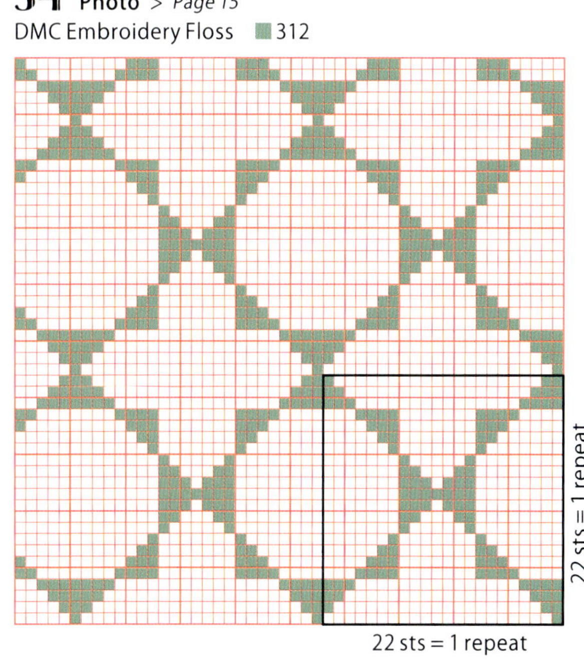

35 Photo > *Page 15*

DMC Embroidery Floss ■ 312

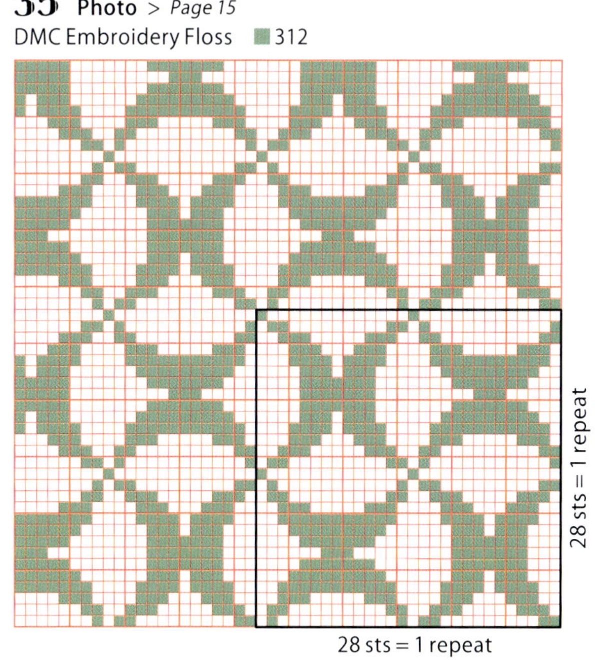

PART TWO

Retro Patterns

Take a step back in time with these patterns inspired by the past. You'll find a variety of motifs featuring retro design elements, such as stripes, starbursts and waves.

37 Instructions > page 34

38 Instructions > page 34

39 Instructions > page 34

40 Instructions > page 34

41 Instructions > page 35

42 Instructions > page 35

43 Instructions > page 35

44 Instructions > page 35

45 Instructions > page 36

46 Instructions > page 36

47 Instructions > page 36

48 Instructions > page 36

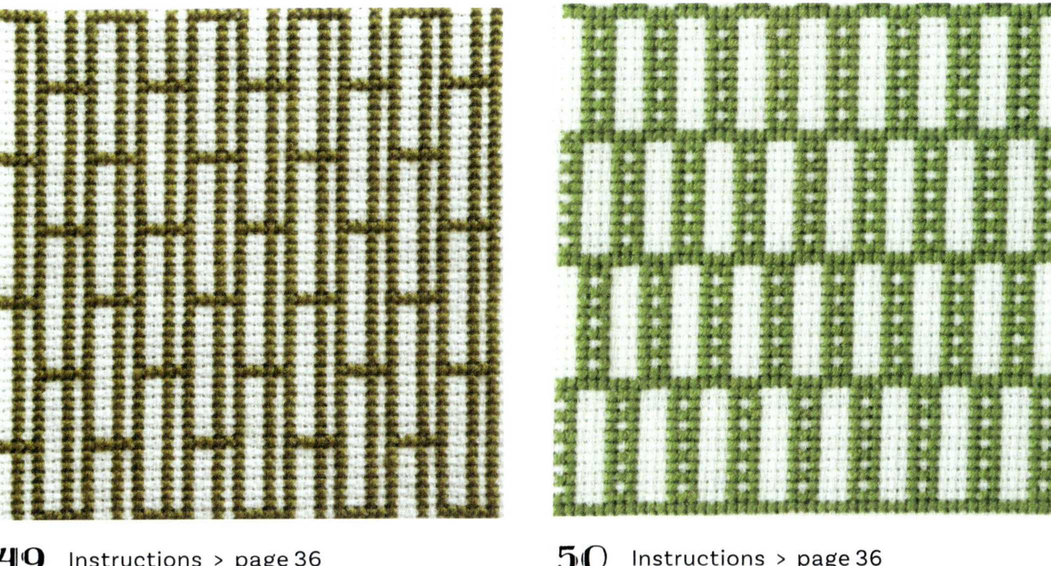

49 Instructions > page 36

50 Instructions > page 36

51 Instructions > page 37

52 Instructions > page 37

53 Instructions > page 37

54 Instructions > page 37

55 Instructions > page 37

56 Instructions > page 37

57 Instructions > page 38

58 Instructions > page 38

59 Instructions > page 38

60 Instructions > page 38

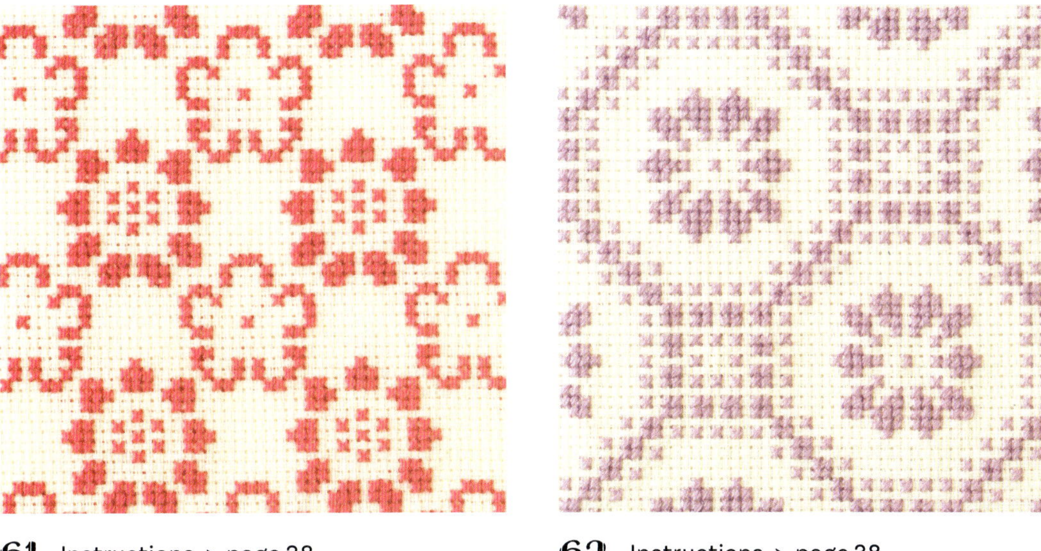

61 Instructions > page 38

62 Instructions > page 38

63 Instructions > page 39

64 Instructions > page 39

65 Instructions > page 39

66 Instructions > page 39

Experimenting with Colour Schemes

Simply changing the colour scheme can create a completely different-looking design. In the following examples, we'll experiment with colour placement for two retro motifs.

64 Shown on page 29

First, let's take a look at motif 64 from the previous page. Motif 67 features the same exact colour scheme, but with inverse placement, relying on negative space to create the star pattern. Motifs 68-70 all use purple, pink and green, but different colour placements make the background patterns stand out and create movement within the design.

67

DMC Embroidery Floss ■ 208

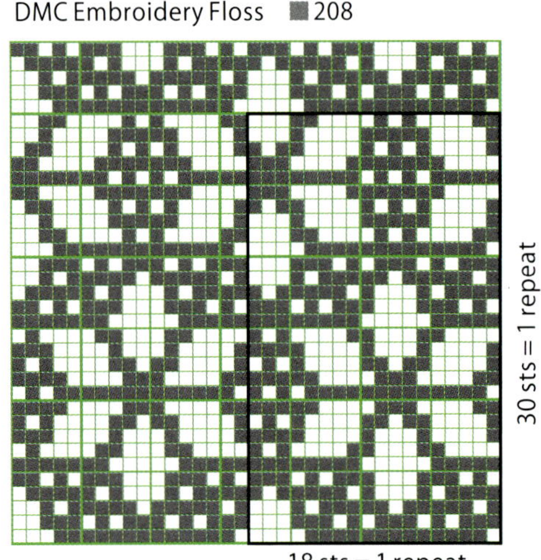

DMC Embroidery Floss ■ 208 ■ 3716 ■ 3364

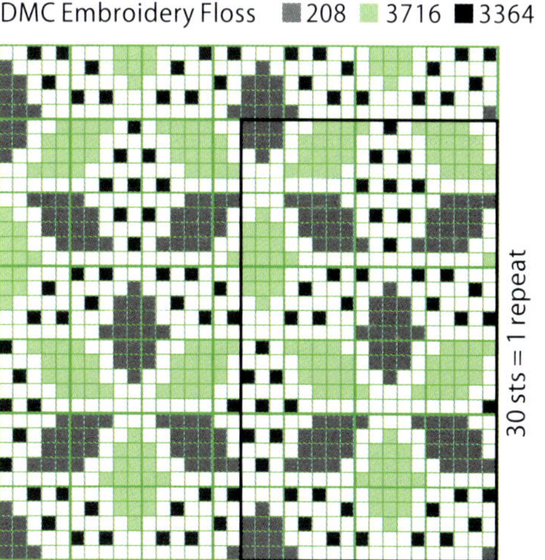

30 sts = 1 repeat

18 sts = 1 repeat

68

DMC Embroidery Floss ■ 208 ■ 3716 ■ 3364

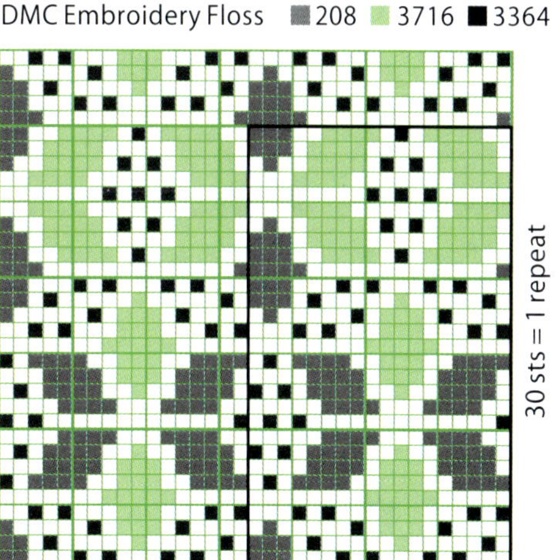

30 sts = 1 repeat

18 sts = 1 repeat

69

DMC Embroidery Floss ■ 208 ■ 3716 ■ 3364

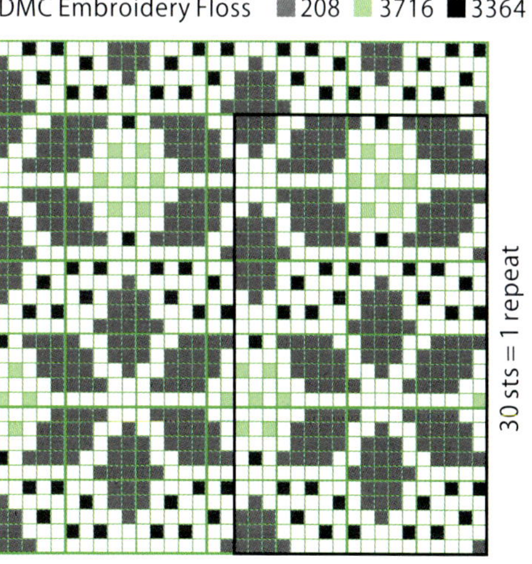

30 sts = 1 repeat

18 sts = 1 repeat

70

47 Shown on page 26

Now let's experiment with motif 47. Motif 71 features the same colour scheme, but with inverse placement. In addition to the white background fabric, motifs 72-74 all feature light green, dark green and maroon. The different colour placements highlight certain elements of the pattern, especially the diamond-shaped borders and vertical lines.

71

DMC Embroidery Floss ■ 734

72

DMC Embroidery Floss ■ 734 ■ 3051 ■ 315

73

74

DMC Embroidery Floss 734 3051 315

26 sts = 1 repeat

26 sts = 1 repeat

37 Photo > *Page 25*

DMC Embroidery Floss ■3364 ■3776

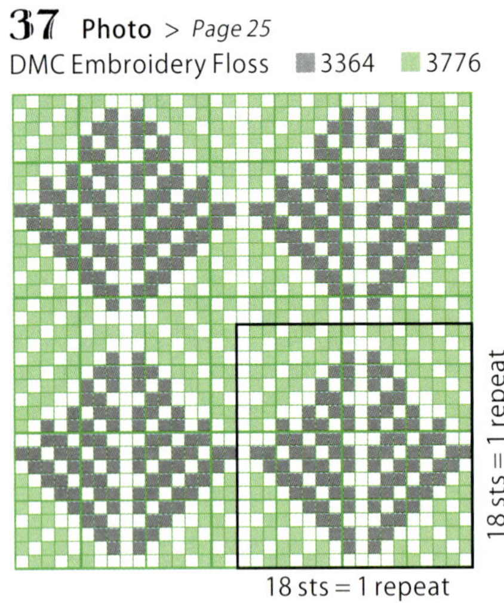

38 Photo > *Page 25*

DMC Embroidery Floss ■799 ■3882

39 Photo > *Page 25*

DMC Embroidery Floss ■304 ■840

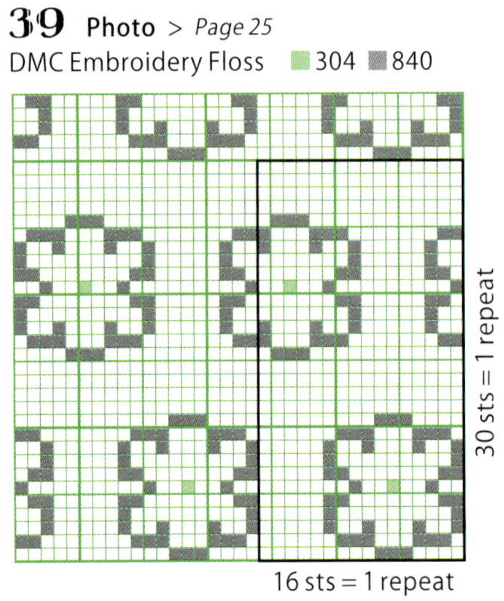

40 Photo > *Page 25*

DMC Embroidery Floss ■400 ■738

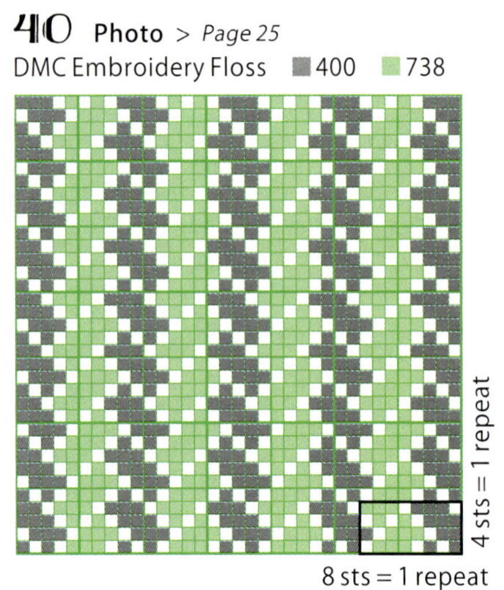

41 Photo > *Page 25*

DMC Embroidery Floss ■ 869 ■ 3819

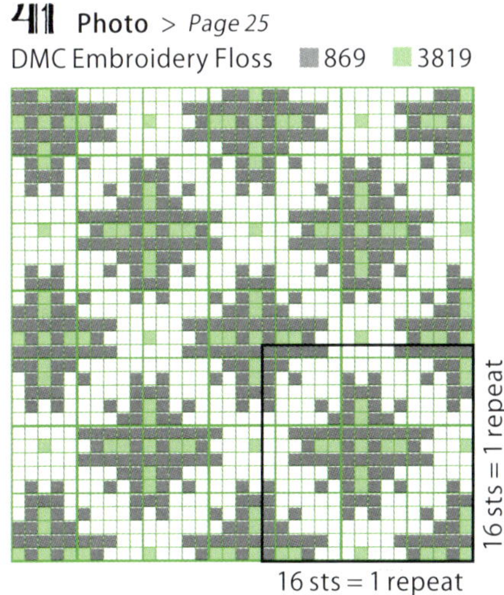

16 sts = 1 repeat

16 sts = 1 repeat

42 Photo > *Page 25*

DMC Embroidery Floss ■ 340 ■ 370

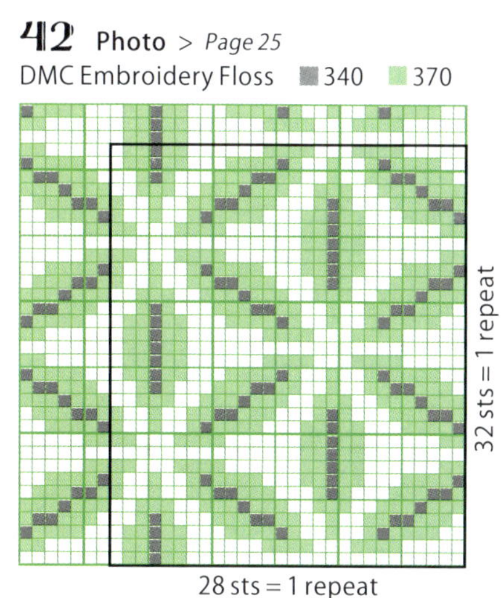

32 sts = 1 repeat

28 sts = 1 repeat

43 Photo > *Page 26*

DMC Embroidery Floss ■ 3854

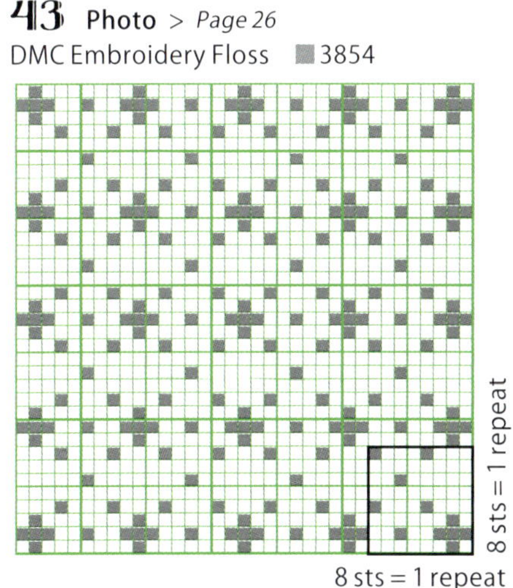

8 sts = 1 repeat

8 sts = 1 repeat

44 Photo > *Page 26*

DMC Embroidery Floss ■ 3852

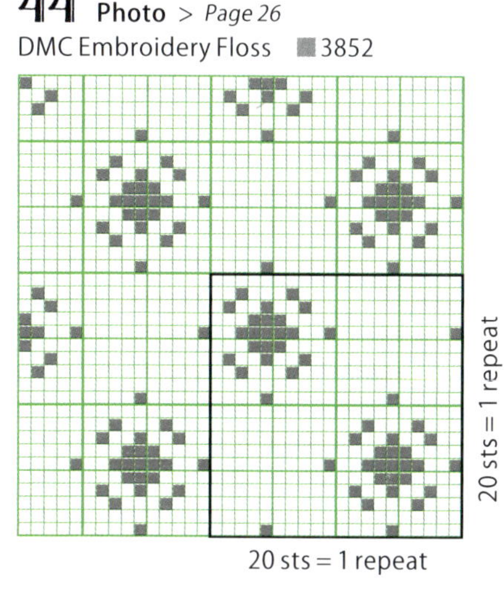

20 sts = 1 repeat

20 sts = 1 repeat

45 Photo > *Page 26*

DMC Embroidery Floss ■ 3822

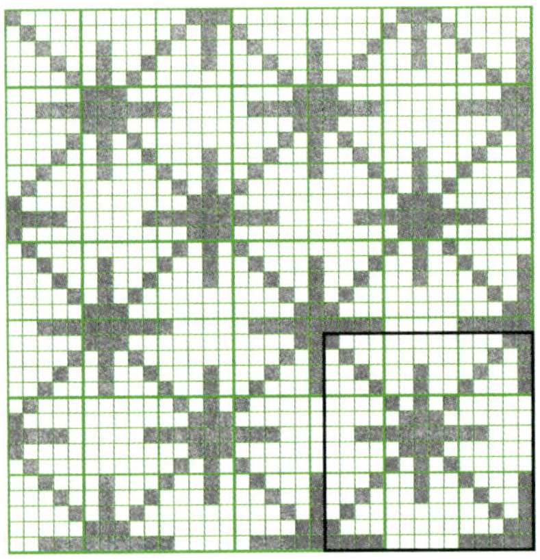

14 sts = 1 repeat

14 sts = 1 repeat

46 Photo > *Page 26*

DMC Embroidery Floss ■ 725

20 sts = 1 repeat

20 sts = 1 repeat

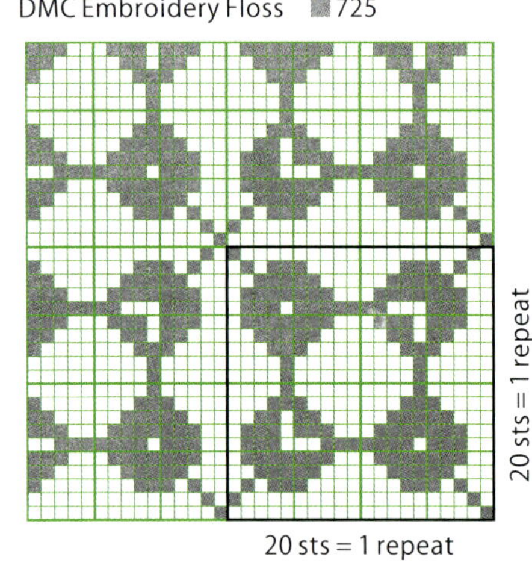

47 Photo > *Page 26*

DMC Embroidery Floss ■ 734

26 sts = 1 repeat

26 sts = 1 repeat

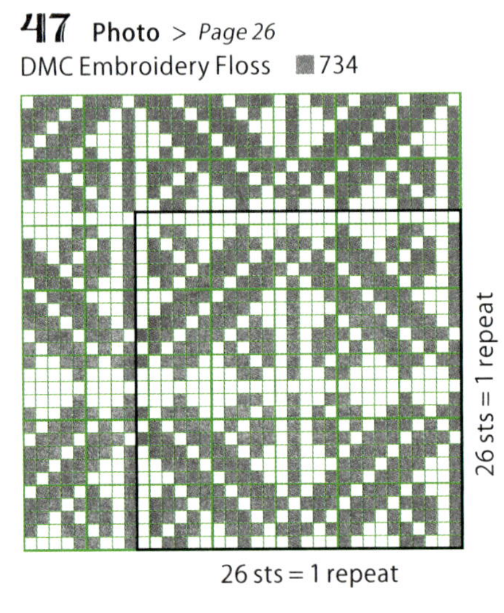

48 Photo > *Page 26*

DMC Embroidery Floss ■ 165

16 sts = 1 repeat

16 sts = 1 repeat

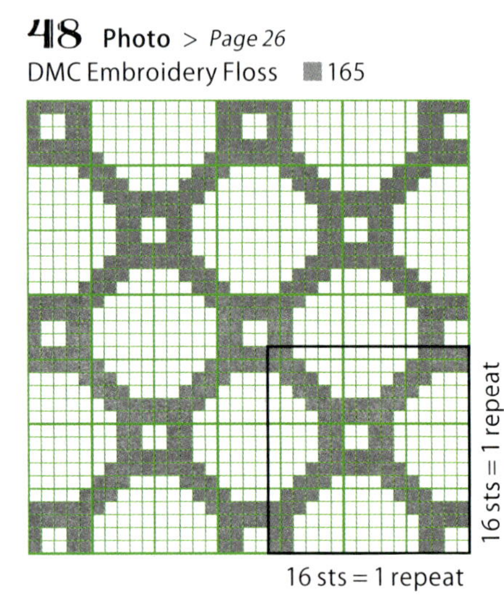

49 Photo > *Page 27*

DMC Embroidery Floss ■ 732

14 sts = 1 repeat

10 sts = 1 repeat

50 Photo > *Page 27*

DMC Embroidery Floss ■ 471

24 sts = 1 repeat

6 sts = 1 repeat

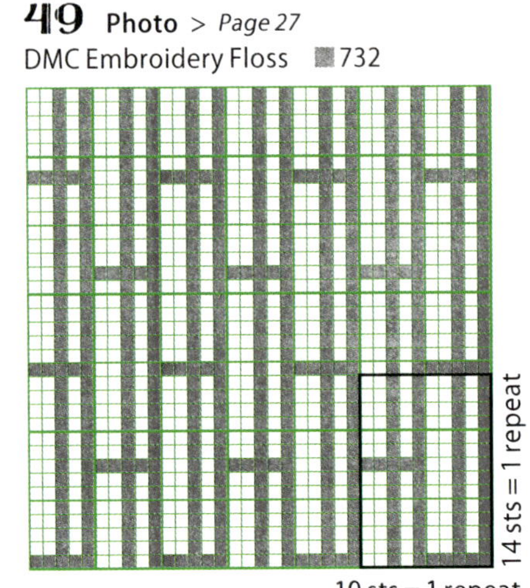

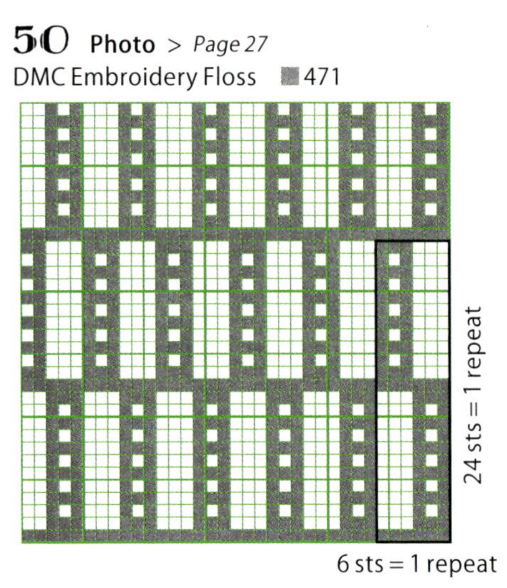

51 Photo > *Page 27*

DMC Embroidery Floss ■ 520

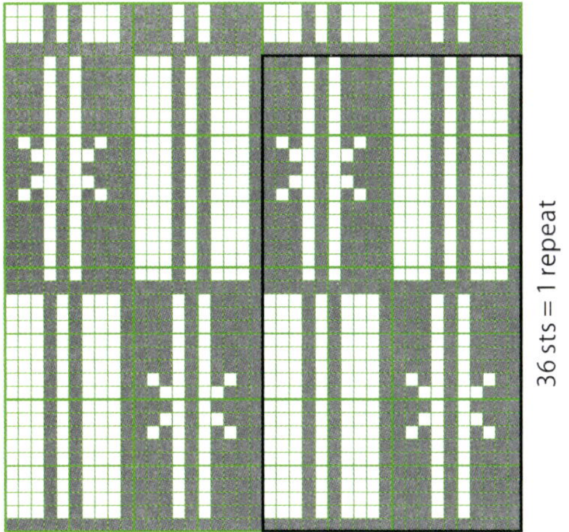

52 Photo > *Page 27*

DMC Embroidery Floss ■ 907

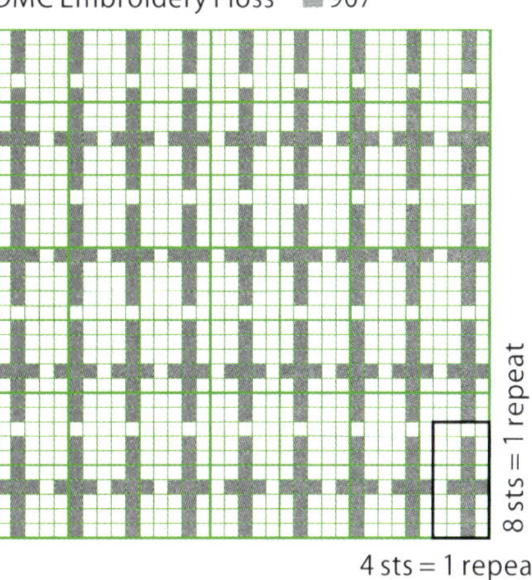

53 Photo > *Page 27*

DMC Embroidery Floss ■ 561

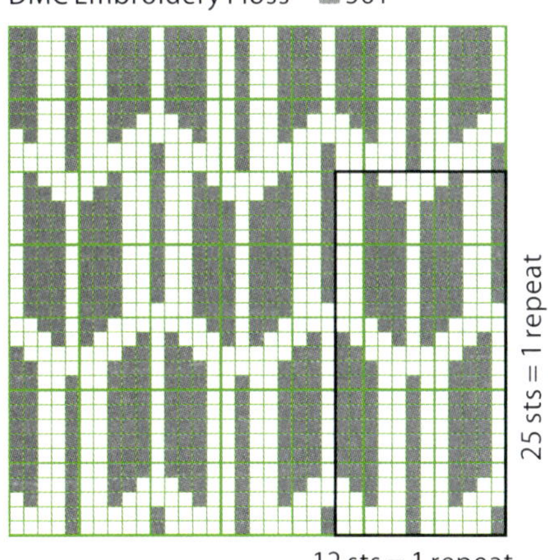

54 Photo > *Page 27*

DMC Embroidery Floss ■ 966

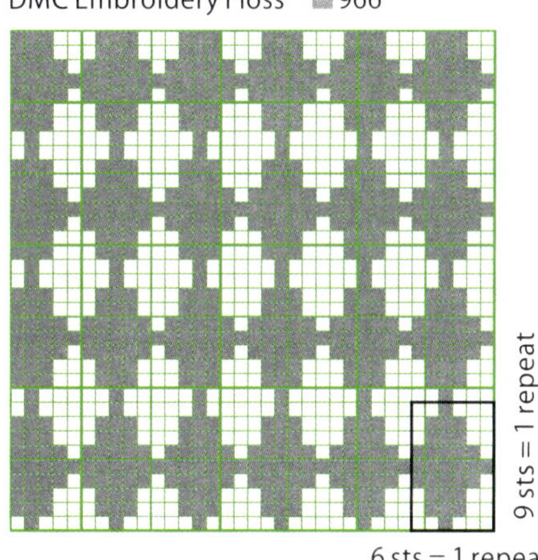

55 Photo > *Page 28*

DMC Embroidery Floss ■ 747

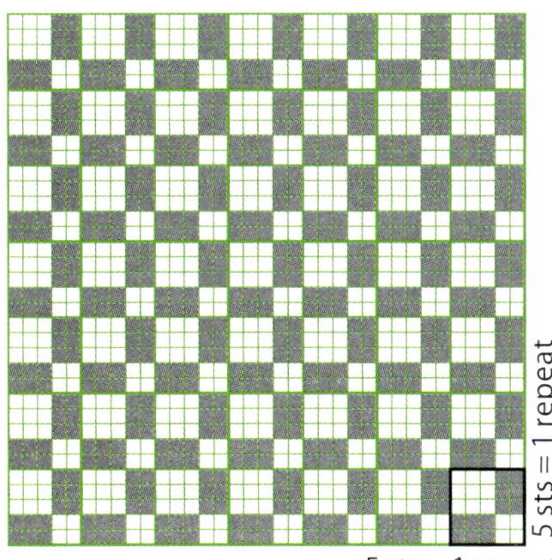

56 Photo > *Page 28*

DMC Embroidery Floss ■ 807

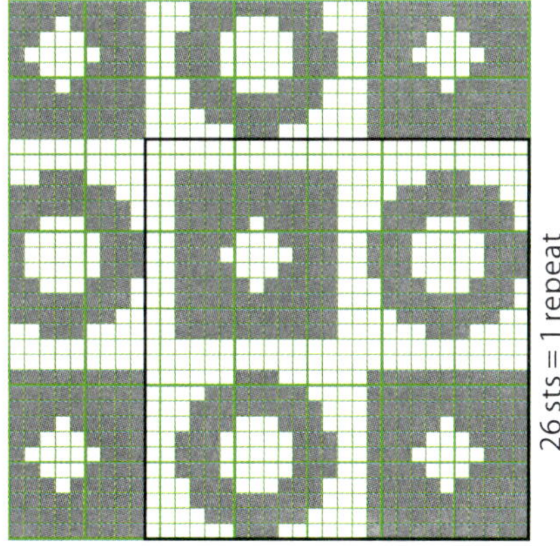

57 Photo > *Page 28*

DMC Embroidery Floss ■ 798

12 sts = 1 repeat

12 sts = 1 repeat

58 Photo > *Page 28*

DMC Embroidery Floss ■ 930

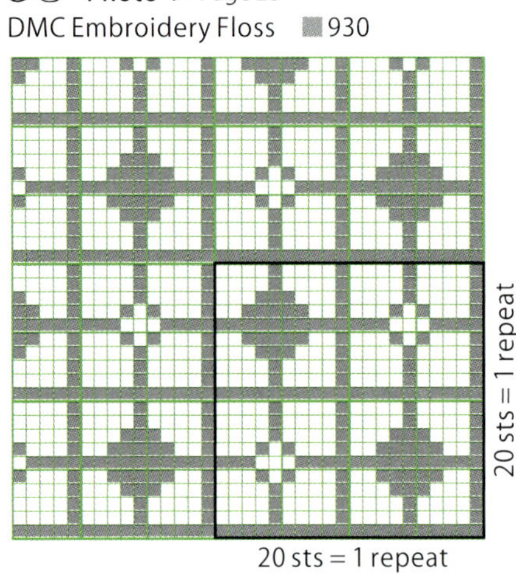

59 Photo > *Page 28*

DMC Embroidery Floss ■ 3760

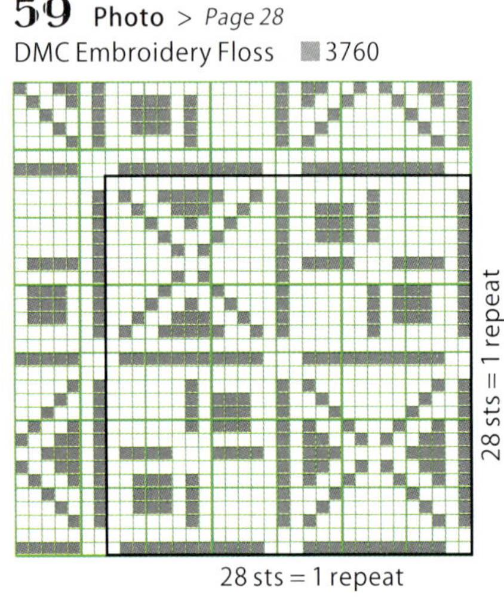

60 Photo > *Page 28*

DMC Embroidery Floss ■ 3761

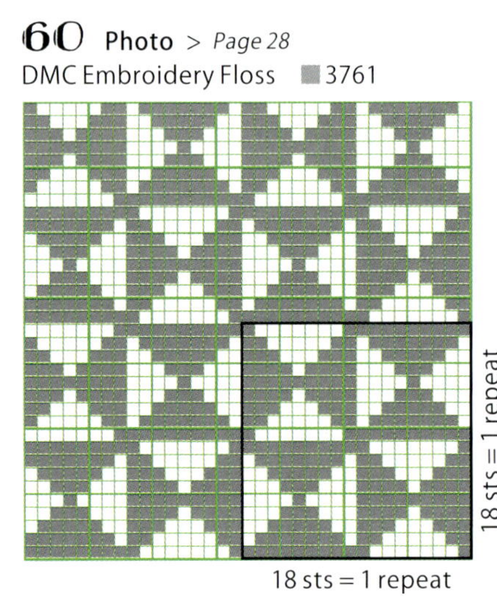

61 Photo > *Page 29*

DMC Embroidery Floss ■ 3805

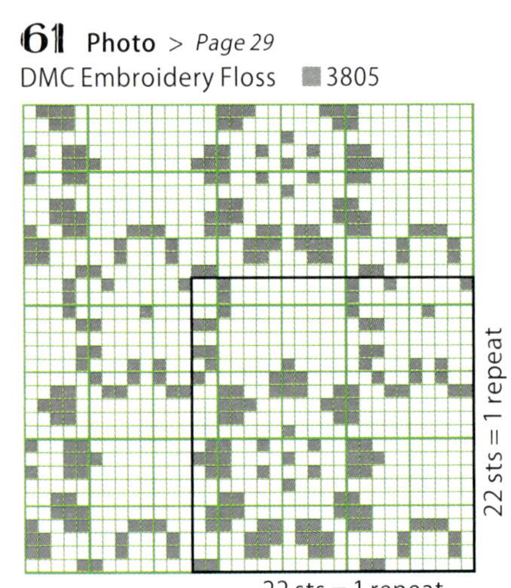

62 Photo > *Page 29*

DMC Embroidery Floss ■ 554

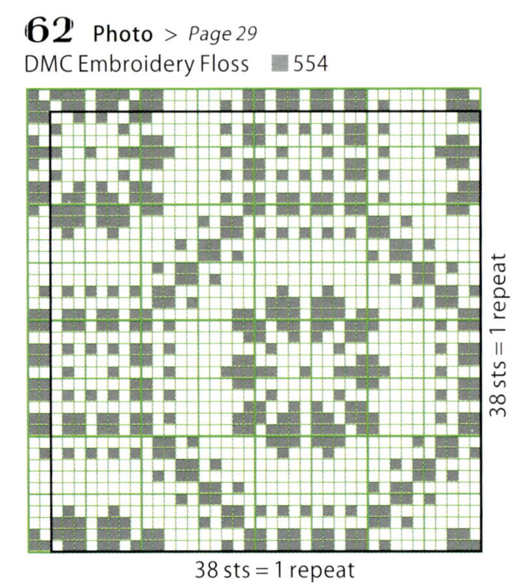

63 Photo > *Page 29*

DMC Embroidery Floss ■155

64 Photo > *Page 29*

DMC Embroidery Floss ■208

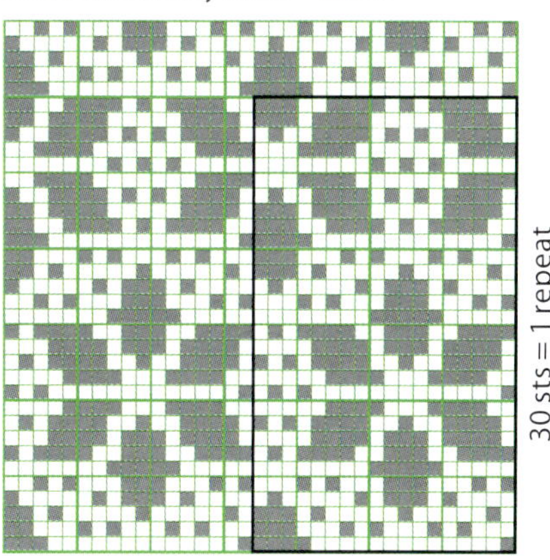

65 Photo > *Page 29*

DMC Embroidery Floss ■550

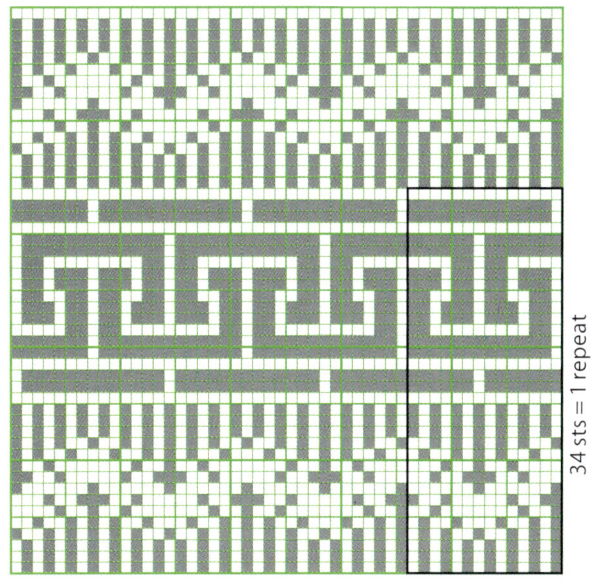

66 Photo > *Page 29*

DMC Embroidery Floss ■3041

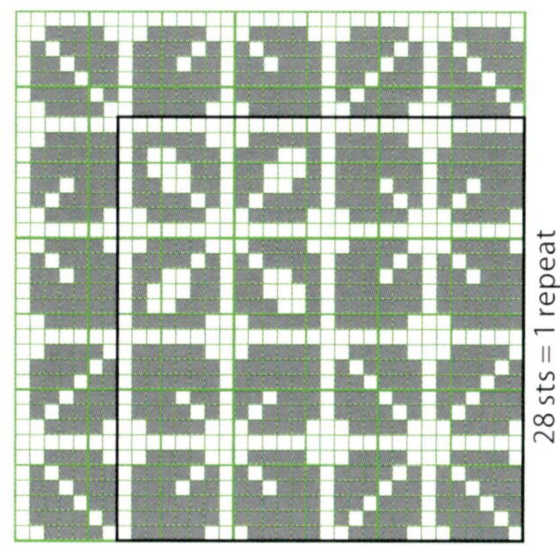

PART THREE

Traditional Japanese Patterns

This collection features patterns that have been popular in Japan for centuries. You'll find patterns that are often seen on kimonos and traditional indigo patterns.

75 Instructions > page 50

76 Instructions > page 50

77 Instructions > page 50

78 Instructions > page 50

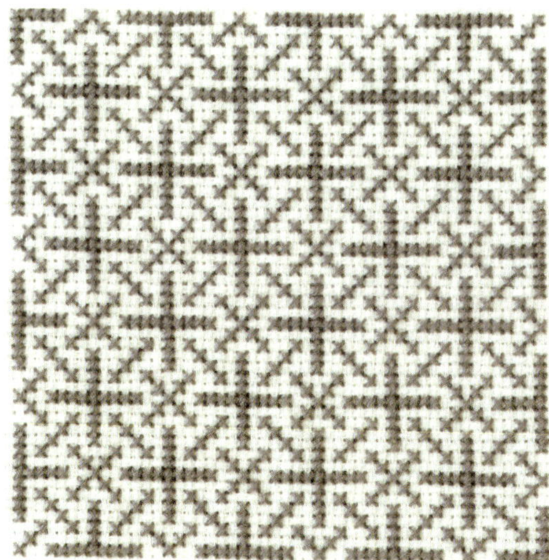

79 Instructions > page 50

80 Instructions > page 50

81 Instructions > page 51

82 Instructions > page 51

83 Instructions > page 51

84 Instructions > page 51

85 Instructions > page 51

86 Instructions > page 52

87 Instructions > page 52

88 Instructions > page 52

89 Instructions > page 52

90 Instructions > page 52

91 Instructions > page 53

92 Instructions > page 53

93 Instructions > page 53

94 Instructions > page 54

95 Instructions > page 54

96 Instructions > page 55

97 Instructions > page 54

98 Instructions > page 54

99 Instructions > page 55

100 Instructions > page 55

101 Instructions > page 55

102 Instructions > page 55

103 Instructions > page 55

104 Instructions > page 55

105 Instructions > page 56

106 Instructions > page 56

107 Instructions > page 56

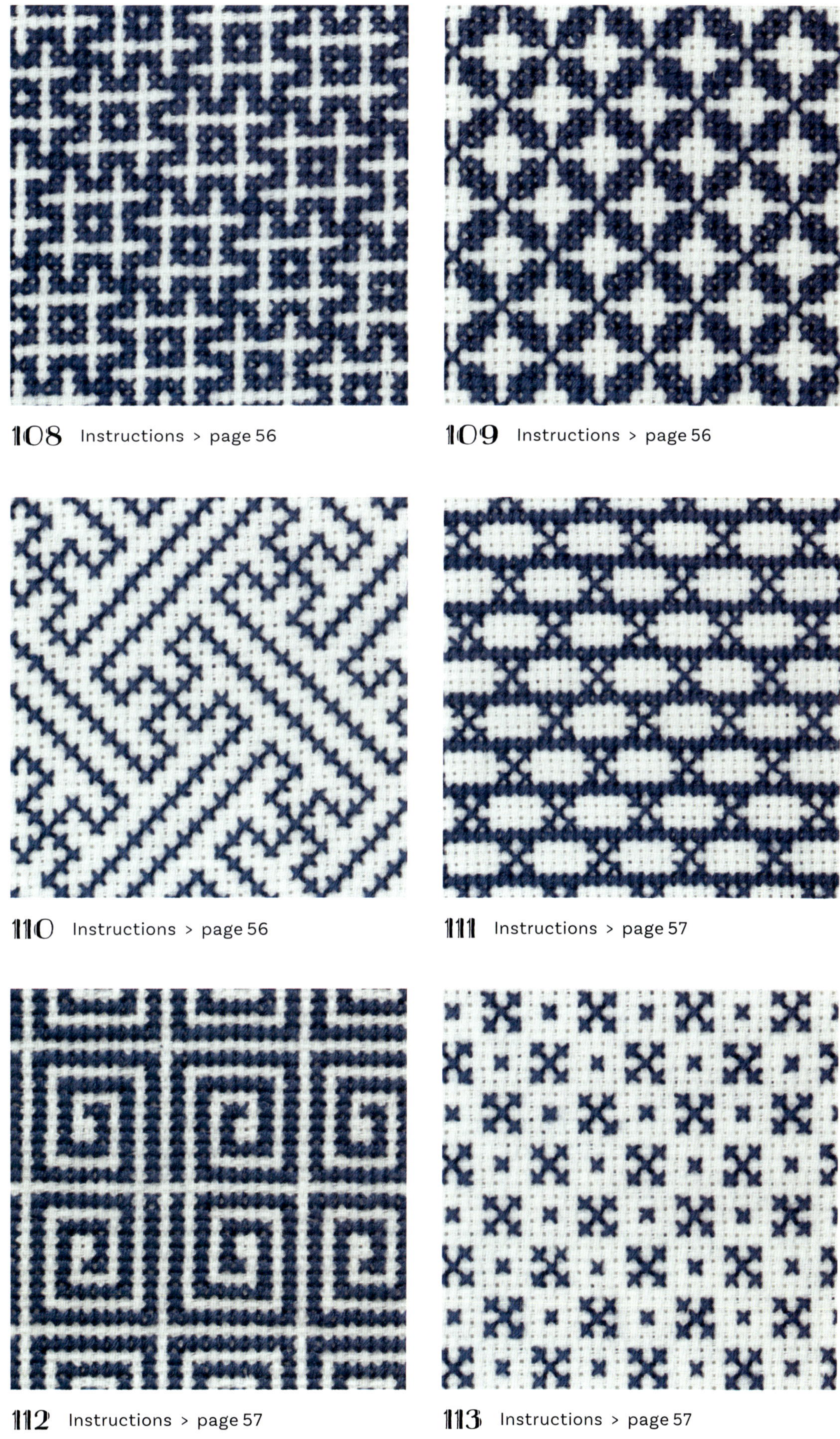

108 Instructions > page 56

109 Instructions > page 56

110 Instructions > page 56

111 Instructions > page 57

112 Instructions > page 57

113 Instructions > page 57

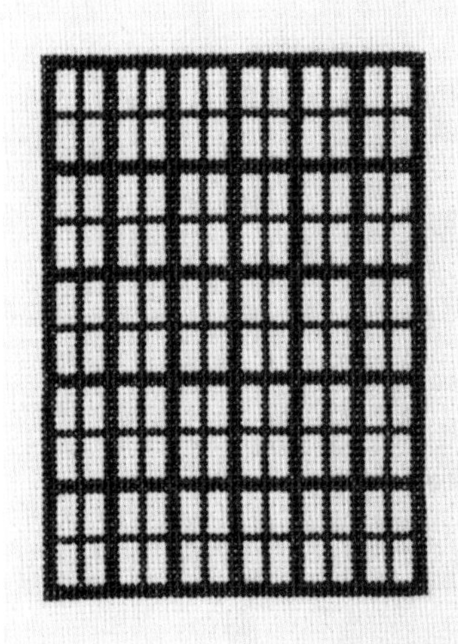

114 Instructions > page 57

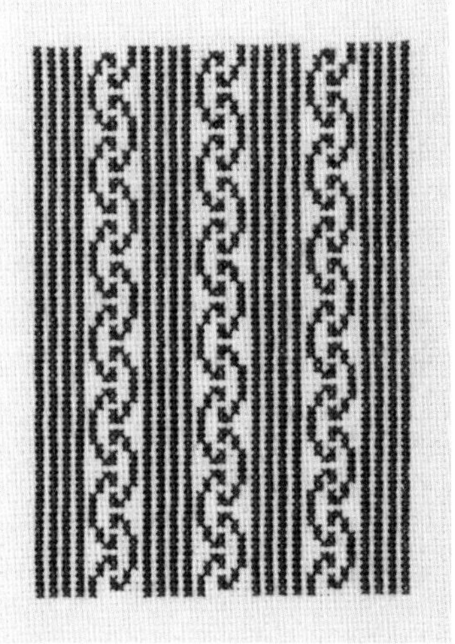

115 Instructions > page 57

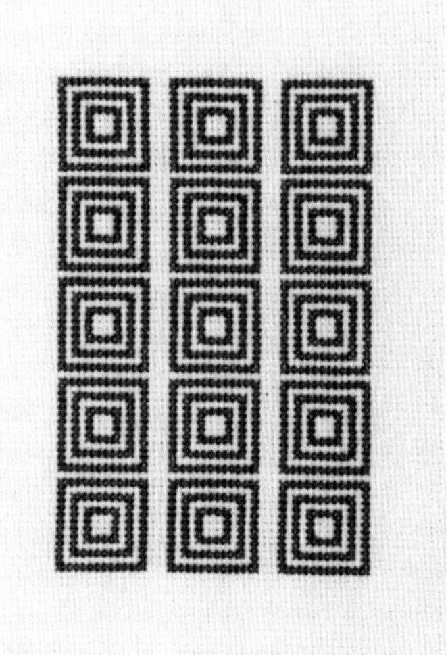

116 Instructions > page 57

117 Instructions > page 58

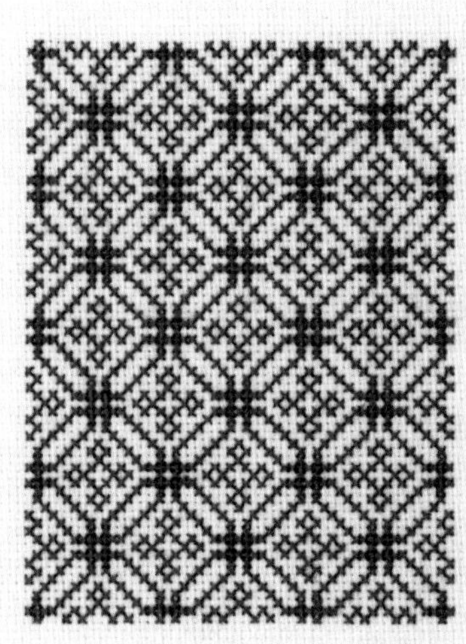

118 Instructions > page 58

119 Instructions > page 58

120 Instructions > page 58

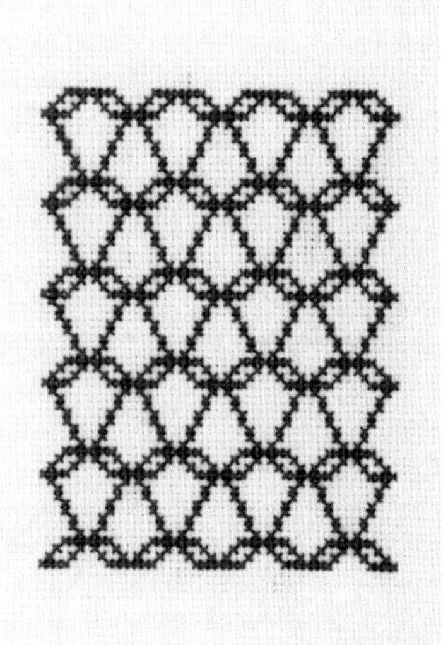

121 Instructions > page 58

122 Instructions > page 58

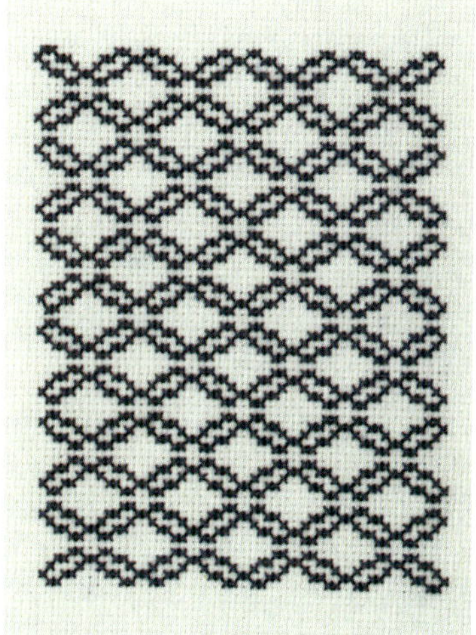

123 Instructions > page 59

124 Instructions > page 59

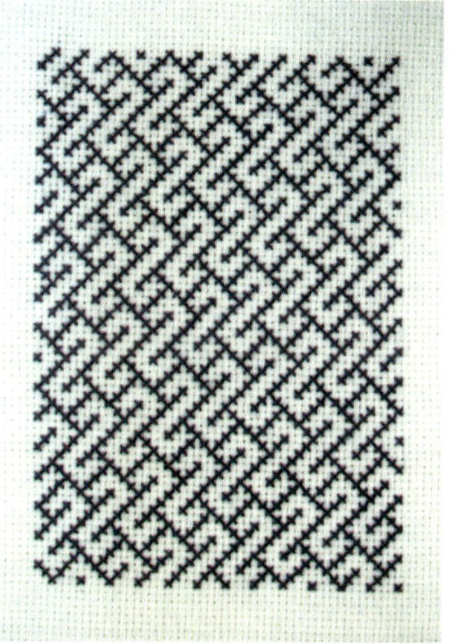

125 Instructions > page 59

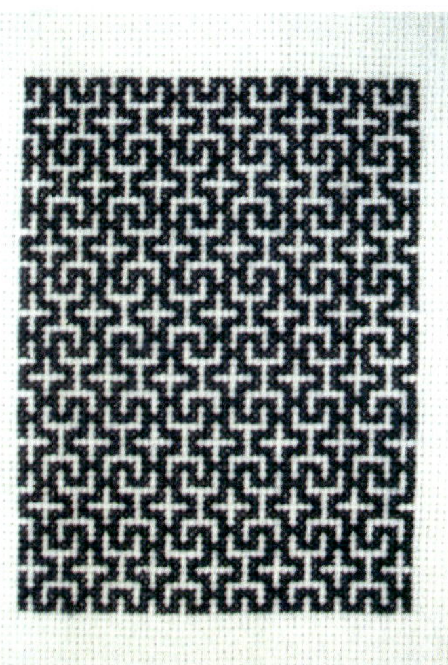

126 Instructions > page 59

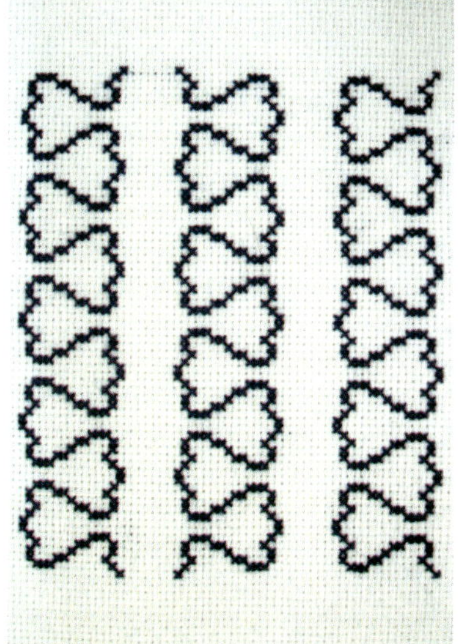

127 Instructions > page 59

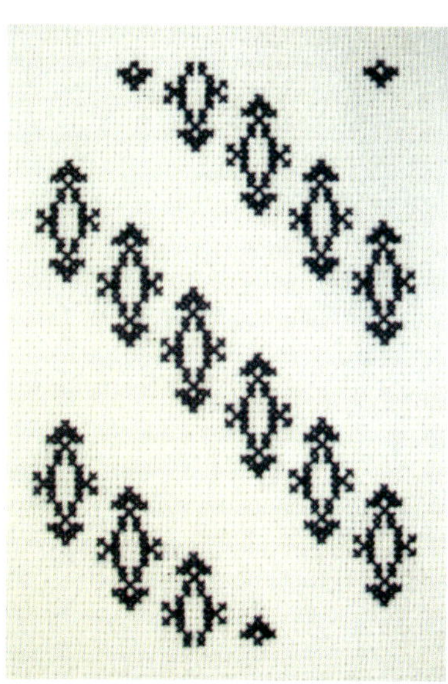

128 Instructions > page 59

75 Photo > *Page 41*

DMC Embroidery Floss ■317

24 sts = 1 repeat

24 sts = 1 repeat

76 Photo > *Page 41*

DMC Embroidery Floss ■932

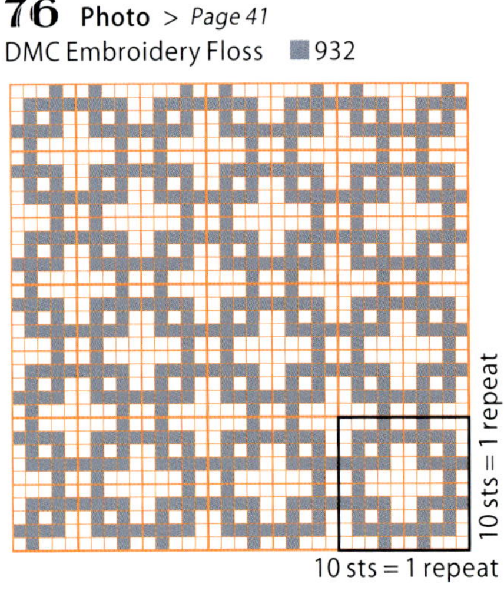

77 Photo > *Page 41*

DMC Embroidery Floss ■647

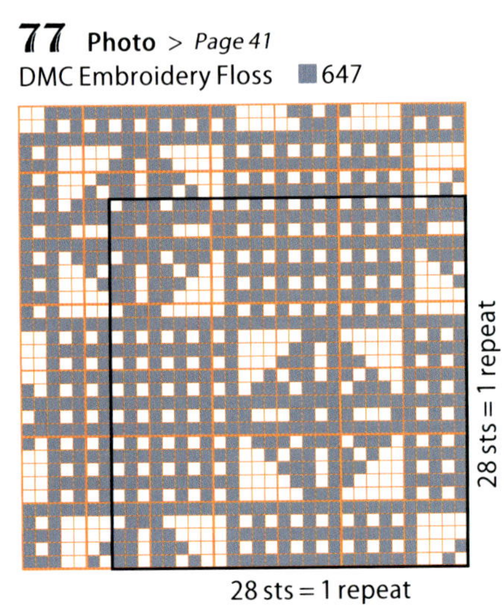

78 Photo > *Page 41*

DMC Embroidery Floss ■451

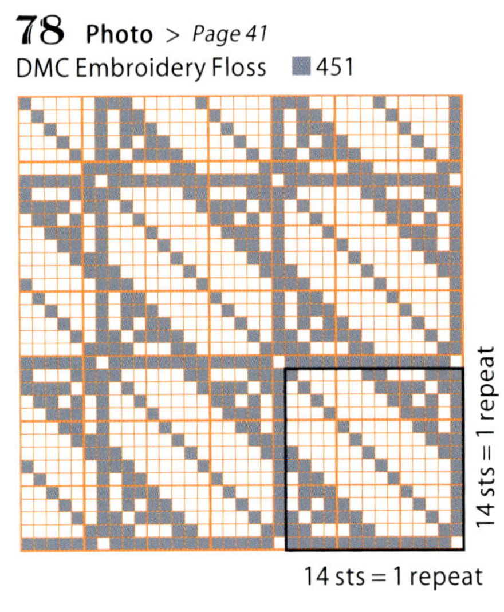

79 Photo > *Page 41*

DMC Embroidery Floss ■414

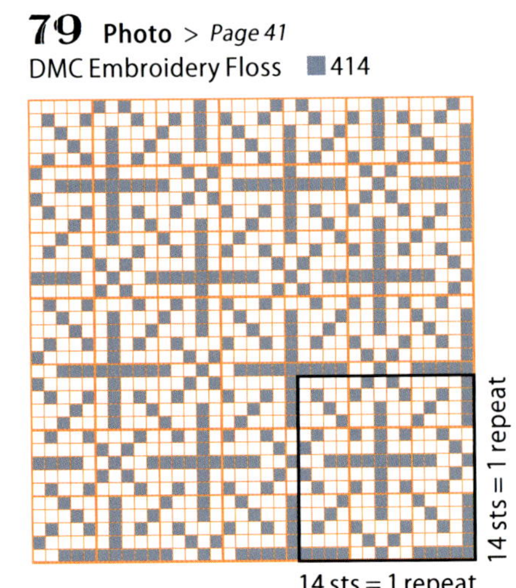

80 Photo > *Page 41*

DMC Embroidery Floss ■646

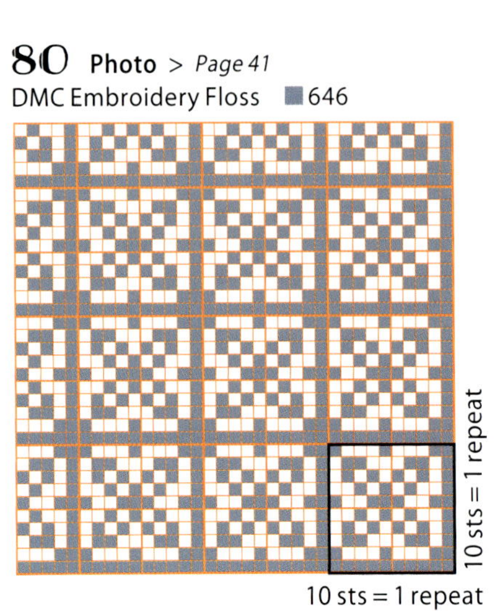

81 Photo > *Page 42*

DMC Embroidery Floss ■ 3328

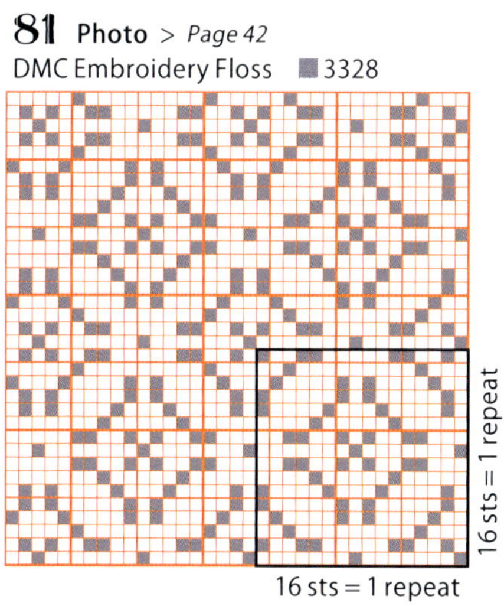

82 Photo > *Page 42*

DMC Embroidery Floss ■ 350

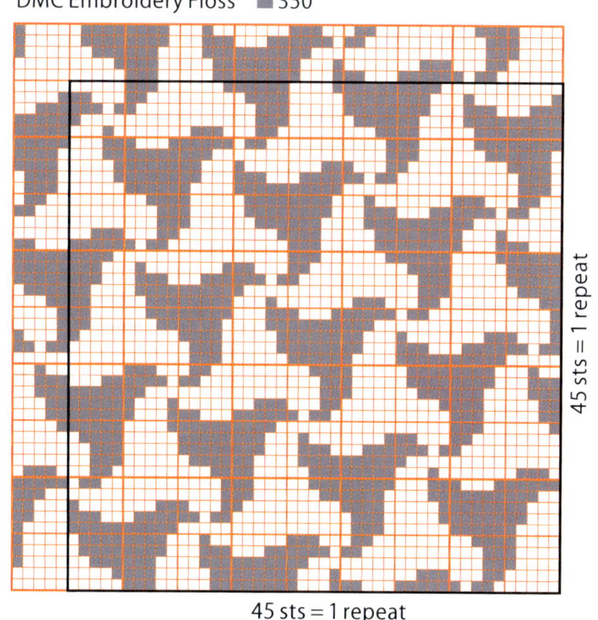

83 Photo > *Page 42*

DMC Embroidery Floss ■ 721

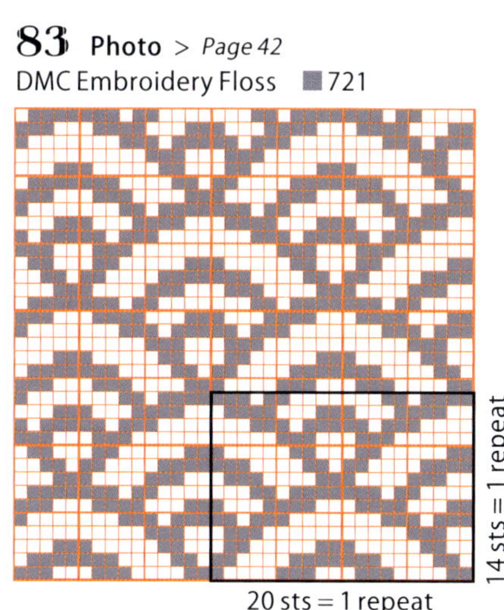

84 Photo > *Page 42*

DMC Embroidery Floss ■ 921

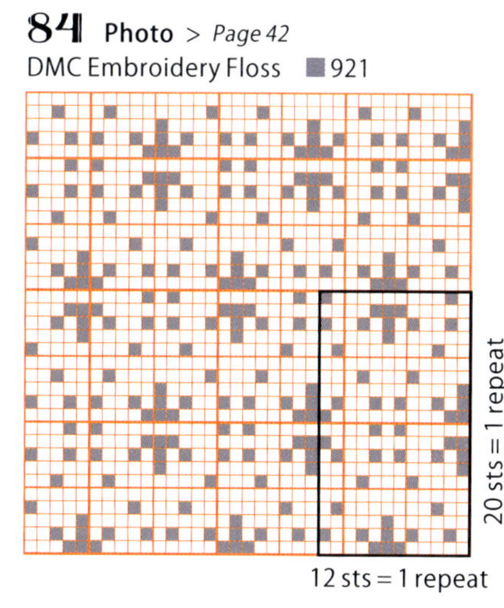

85 Photo > *Page 42*

DMC Embroidery Floss ■ 321

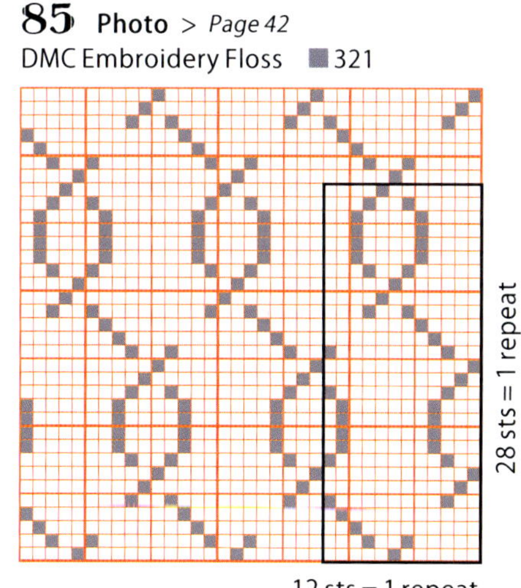

86 Photo > *Page 42*

DMC Embroidery Floss ■3722

91 sts = 1 repeat

35 sts = 1 repeat

87 Photo > *Page 43*

DMC Embroidery Floss ■830

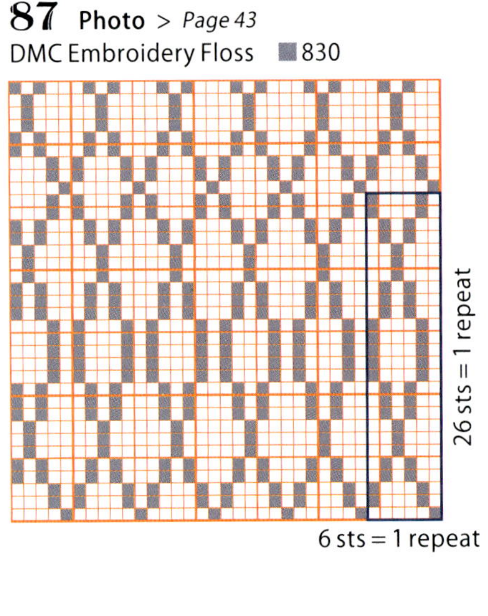

88 Photo > *Page 43*

DMC Embroidery Floss ■433

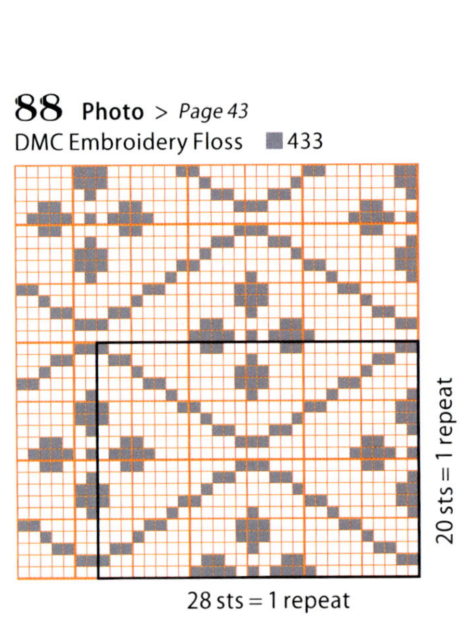

89 Photo > *Page 43*

DMC Embroidery Floss ■221

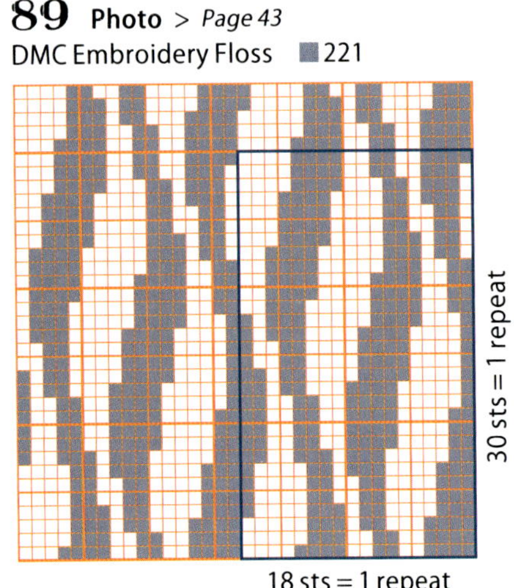

90 Photo > *Page 43*

DMC Embroidery Floss ■838

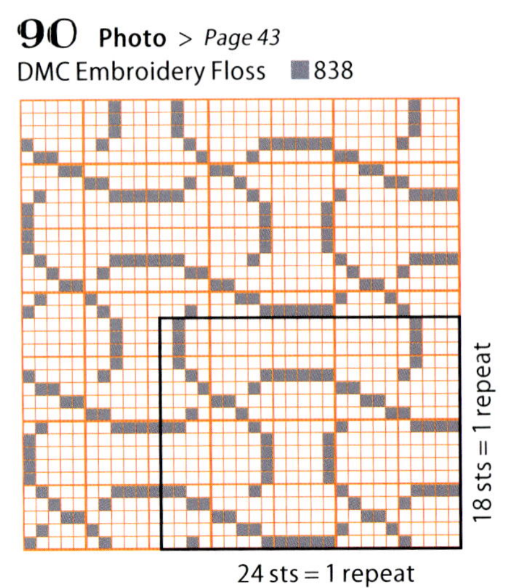

91 Photo > *Page 43*

DMC Embroidery Floss ■ 422

17 sts = 1 repeat

16 sts = 1 repeat

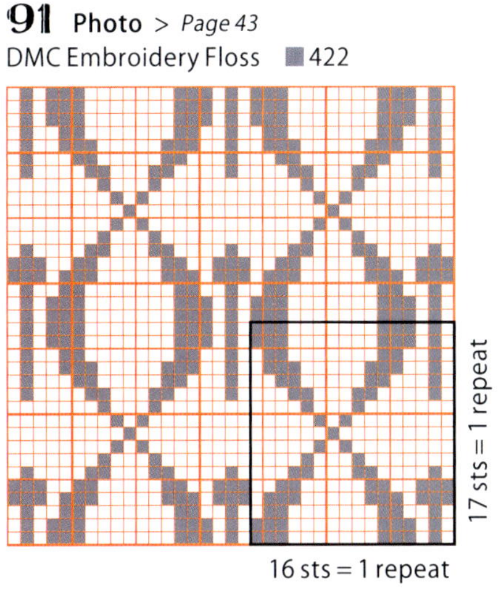

92 Photo > *Page 43*

DMC Embroidery Floss ■ 976

22 sts = 1 repeat

12 sts = 1 repeat

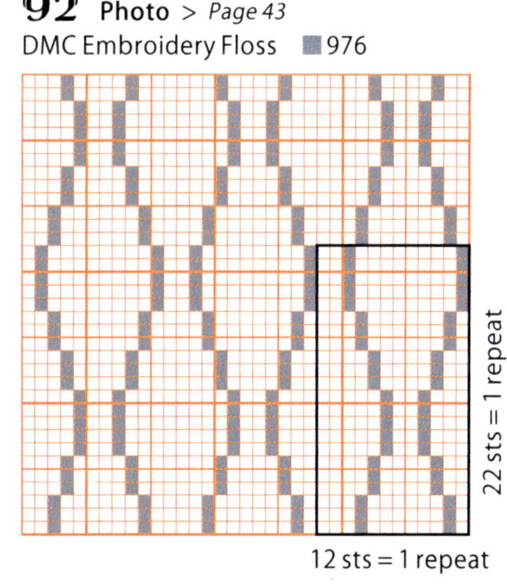

93 Photo > *Page 44*

DMC Embroidery Floss

■ 3832 ■ 761

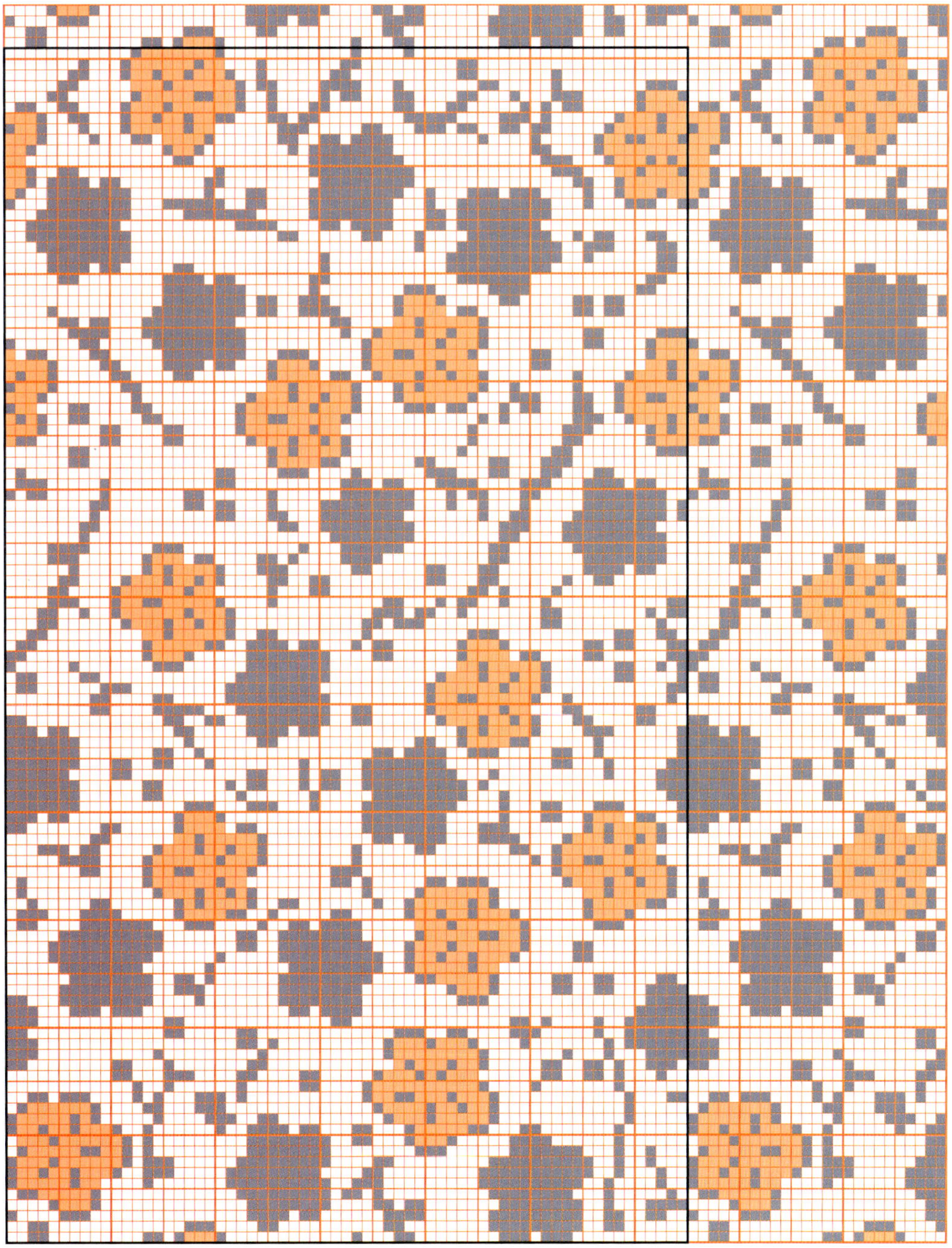

111 sts = 1 repeat

65 sts = 1 repeat

94 **Photo** > *Page 44*

DMC Embroidery Floss ■ 3608

8 sts = 1 repeat

8 sts = 1 repeat

95 **Photo** > *Page 44*

DMC Embroidery Floss ■ 562

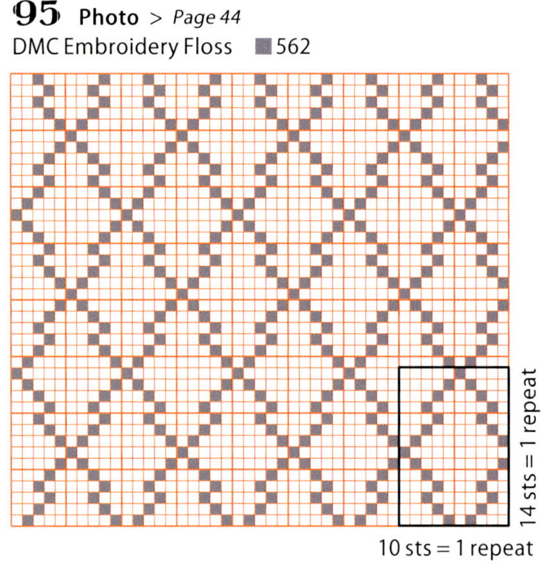

97 **Photo** > *Page 45*

DMC Embroidery Floss ■ 702

98 **Photo** > *Page 45*

DMC Embroidery Floss ■ 742

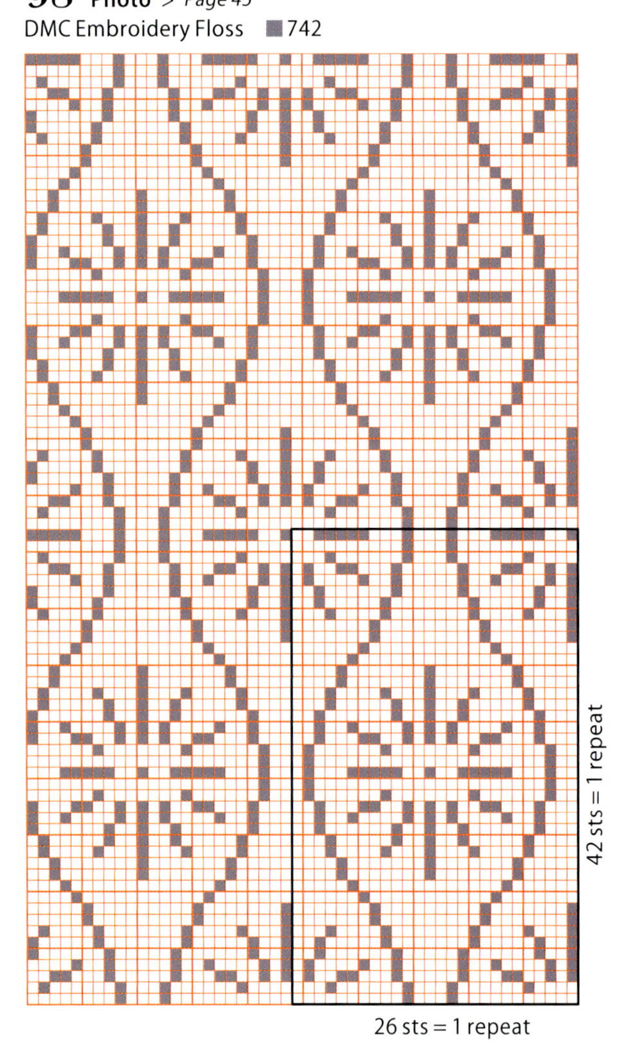

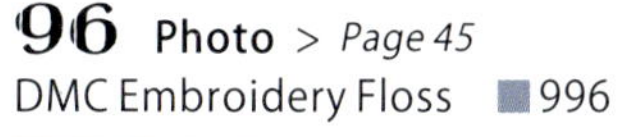

96 Photo > *Page 45*

DMC Embroidery Floss ■ 996

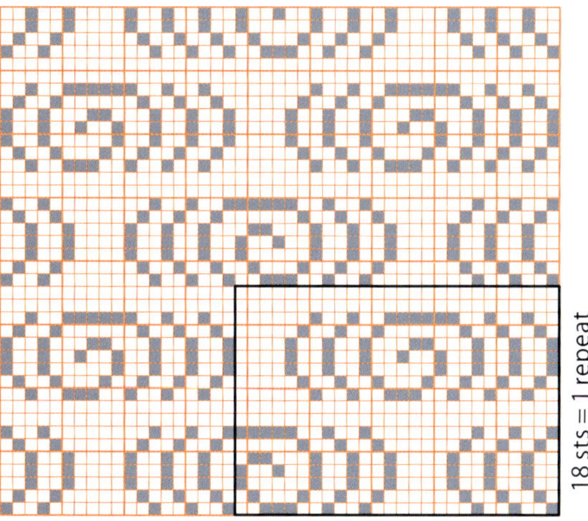

99 Photo > *Page 45*

DMC Embroidery Floss ■ 552

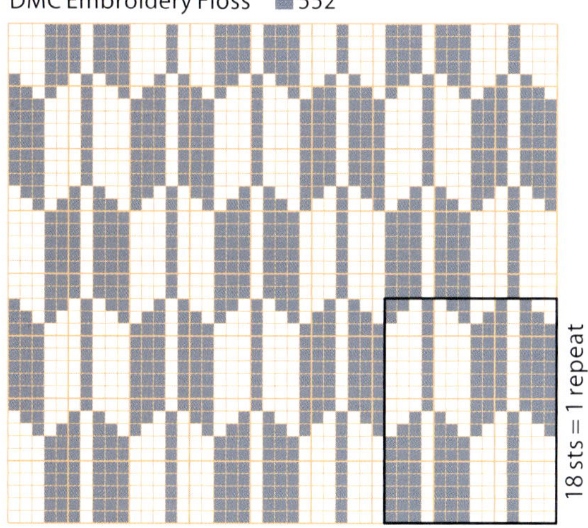

100 Photo > *Page 45*

DMC Embroidery Floss ■ 891

101 Photo > *Page 45*

DMC Embroidery Floss ■ 632

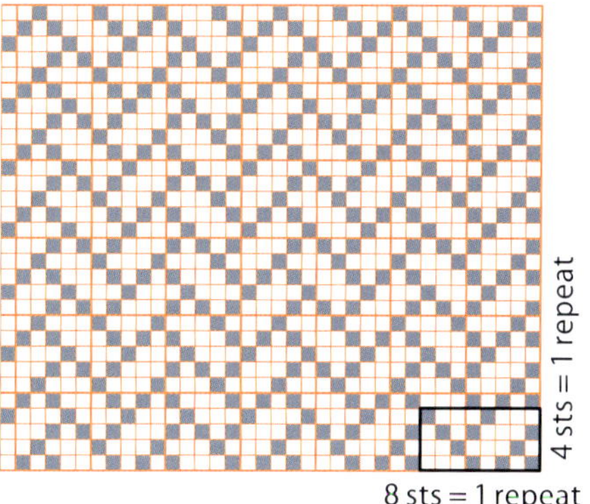

102 Photo > *Page 46*

DMC Embroidery Floss ■ 311

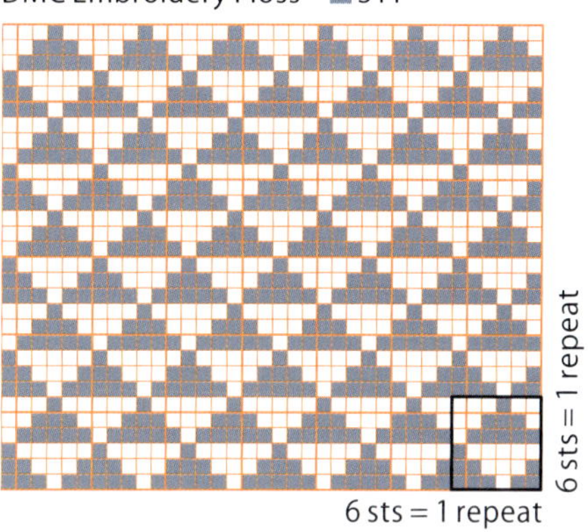

103 Photo > *Page 46*

DMC Embroidery Floss ■ 311

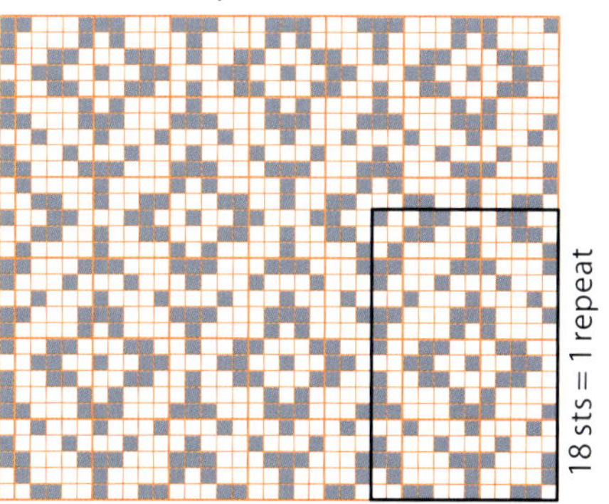

104 Photo > *Page 46*

DMC Embroidery Floss ■ 311

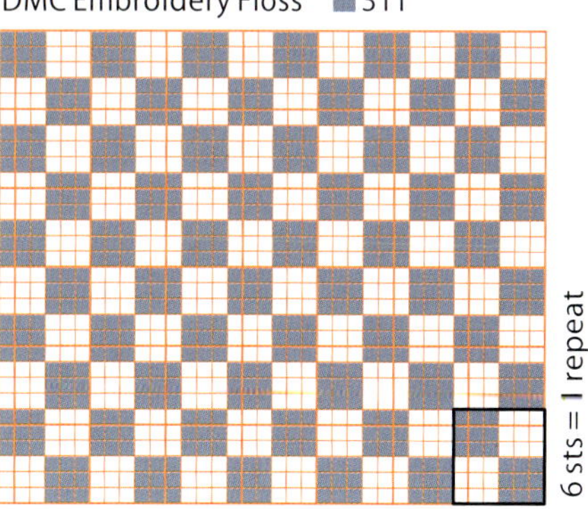

105 **Photo** > *Page 46*

DMC Embroidery Floss ■ 311

12 sts = 1 repeat

6 sts = 1 repeat

106 **Photo** > *Page 46*

DMC Embroidery Floss ■ 311

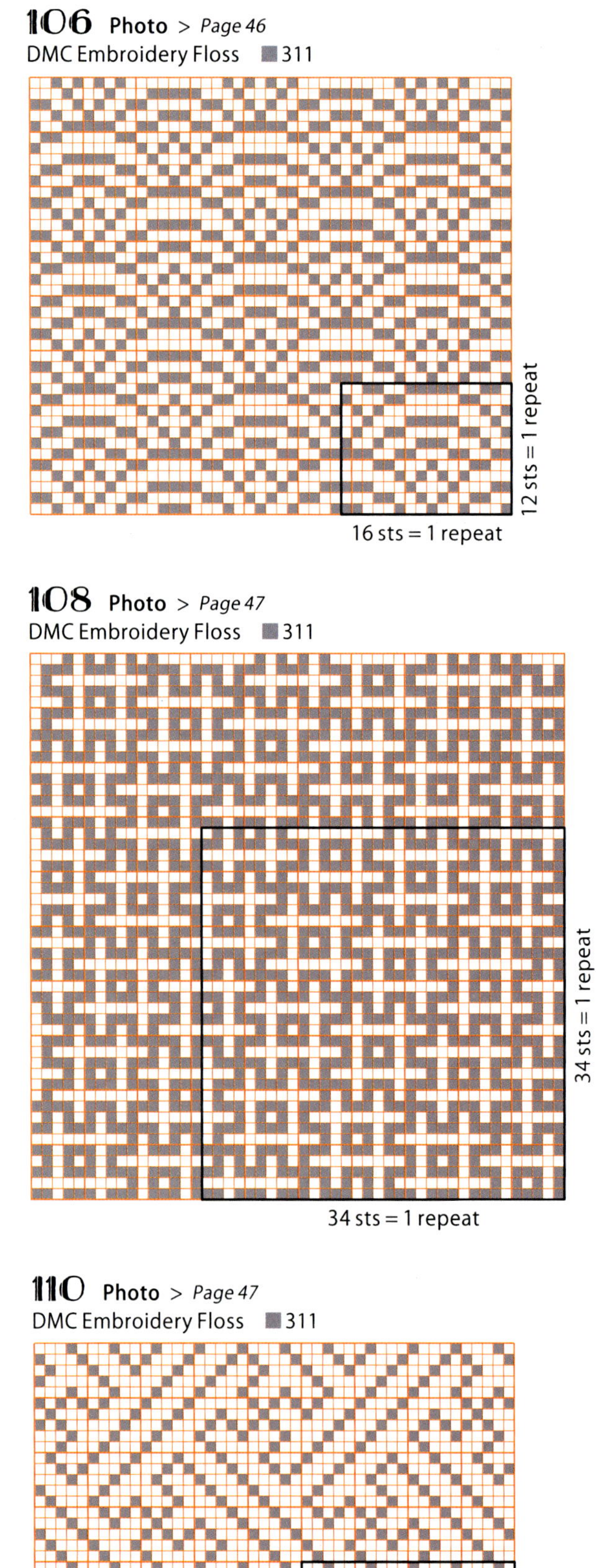

107 **Photo** > *Page 46*

DMC Embroidery Floss ■ 311

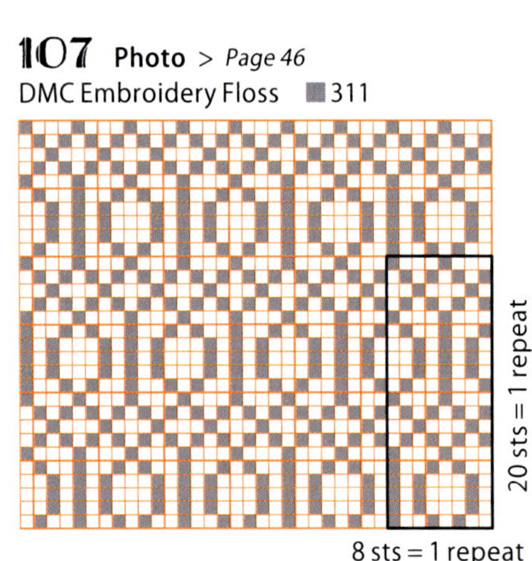

108 **Photo** > *Page 47*

DMC Embroidery Floss ■ 311

109 **Photo** > *Page 47*

DMC Embroidery Floss ■ 311

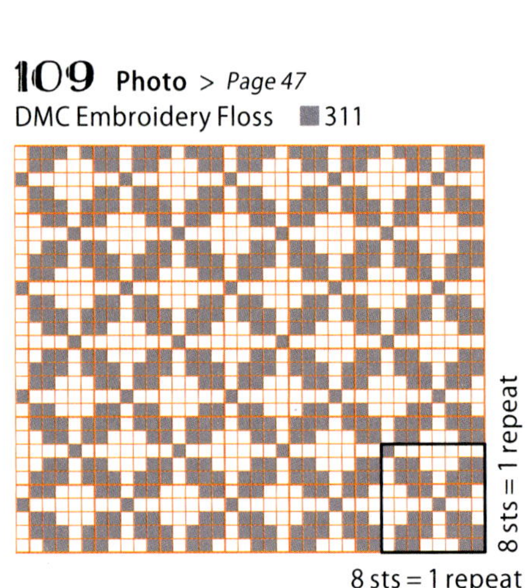

110 **Photo** > *Page 47*

DMC Embroidery Floss ■ 311

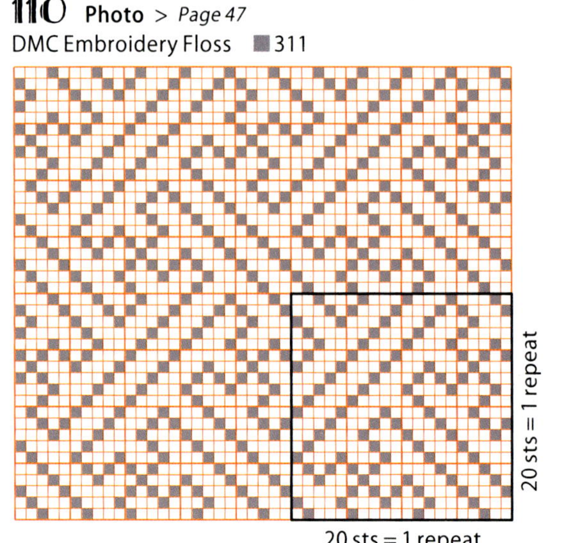

111 **Photo** > *Page 47*

DMC Embroidery Floss ■ 311

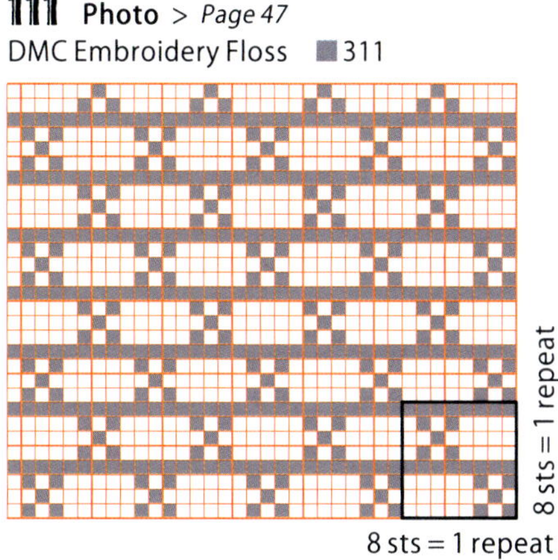

112 **Photo** > *Page 47*

DMC Embroidery Floss ■ 311

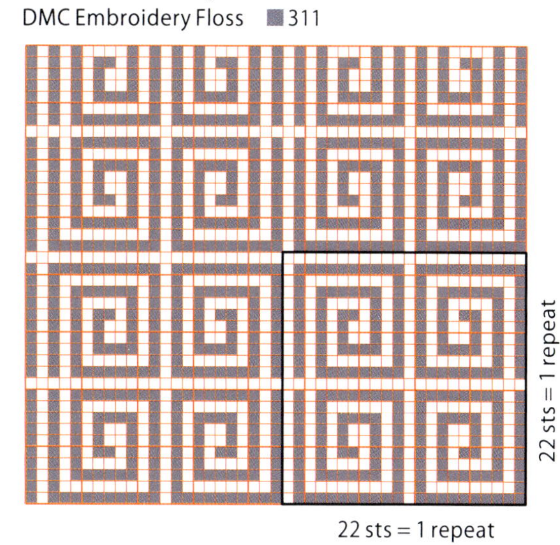

113 **Photo** > *Page 47*

DMC Embroidery Floss ■ 311

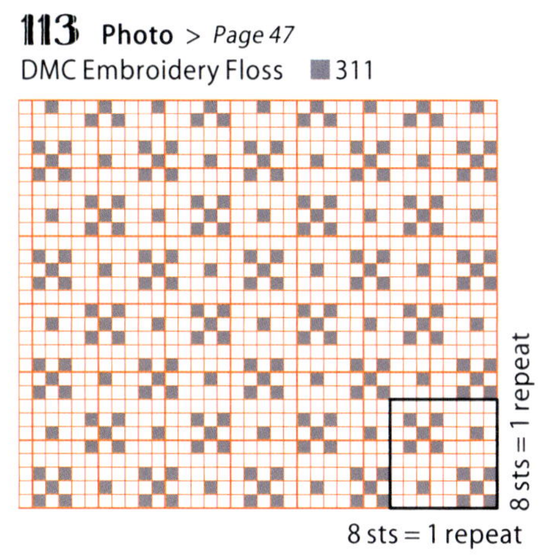

114 **Photo** > *Page 48*

DMC Embroidery Floss ■ 311

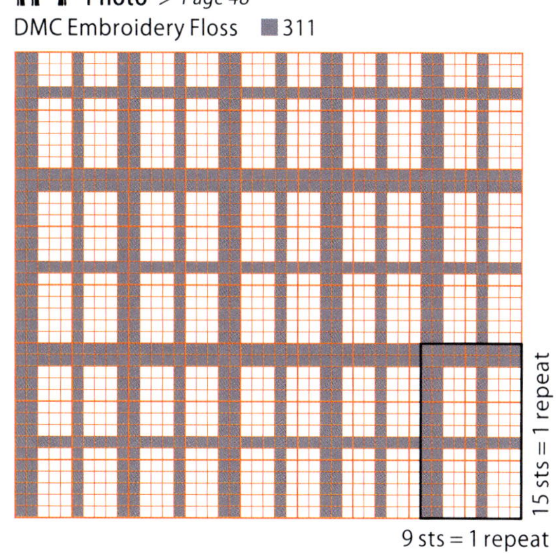

115 **Photo** > *Page 48*

DMC Embroidery Floss ■ 311

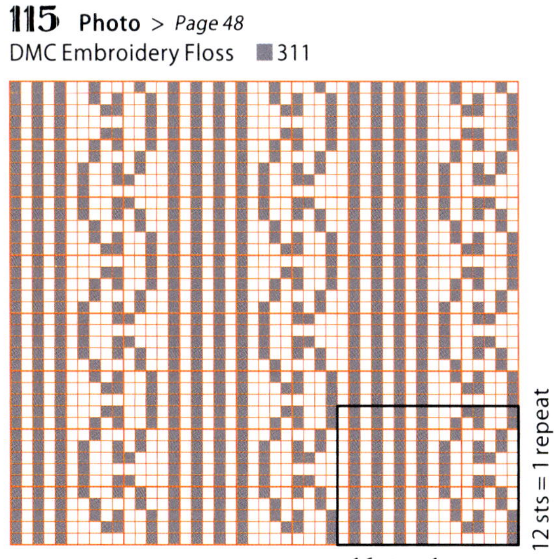

116 **Photo** > *Page 48*

DMC Embroidery Floss ■ 311

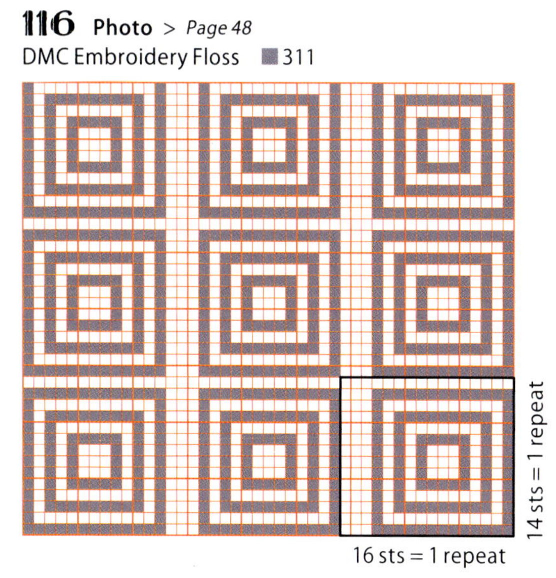

117 Photo > *Page 48*

DMC Embroidery Floss ■311

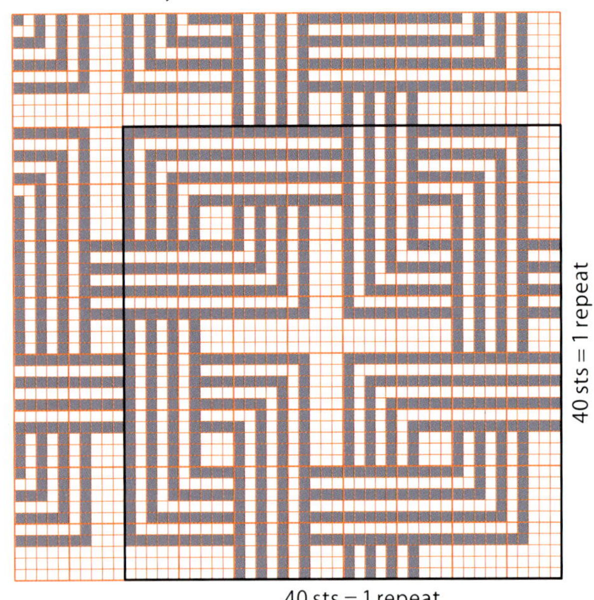

118 Photo > *Page 48*

DMC Embroidery Floss ■311

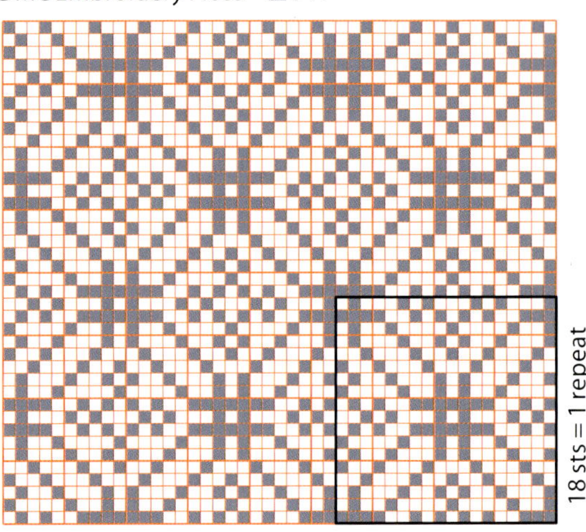

119 Photo > *Page 48*

DMC Embroidery Floss ■311

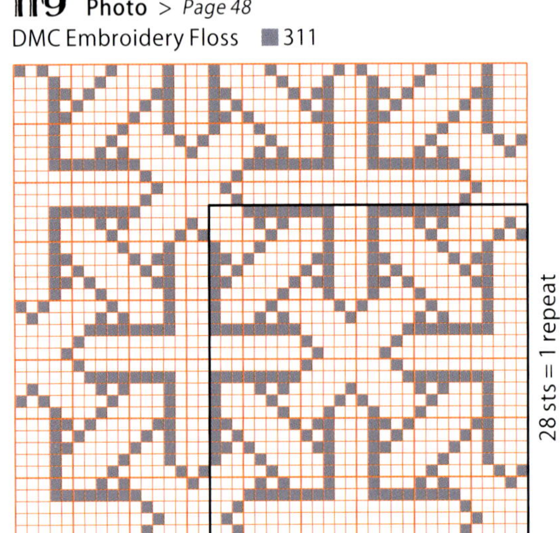

120 Photo > *Page 48*

DMC Embroidery Floss ■311

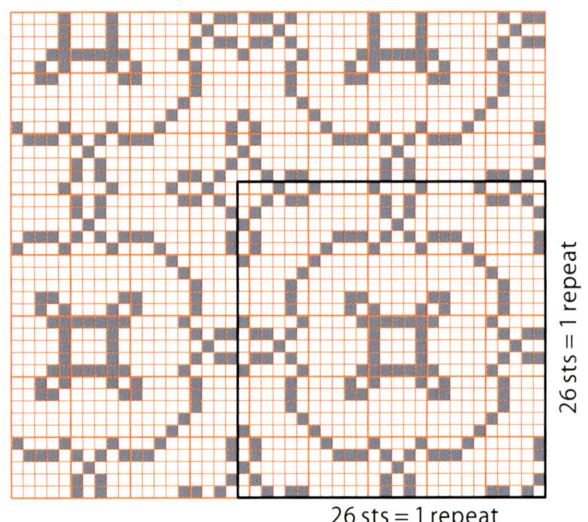

121 Photo > *Page 48*

DMC Embroidery Floss ■311

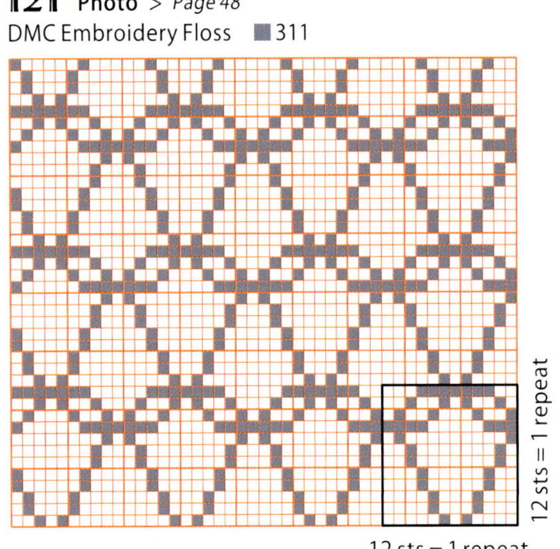

122 Photo > *Page 49*

DMC Embroidery Floss ■311

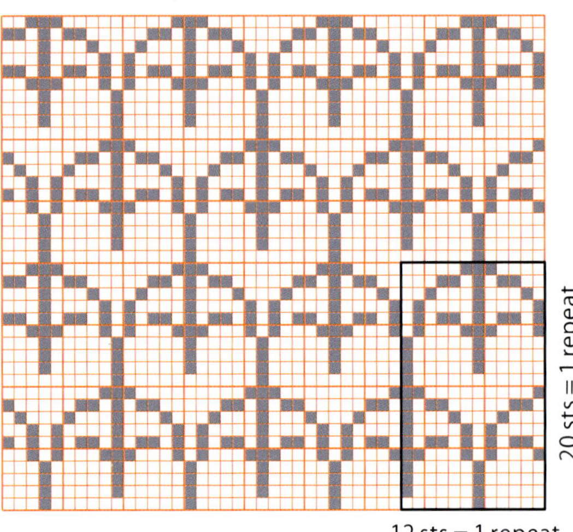

123 Photo > *Page 49*

DMC Embroidery Floss ■311

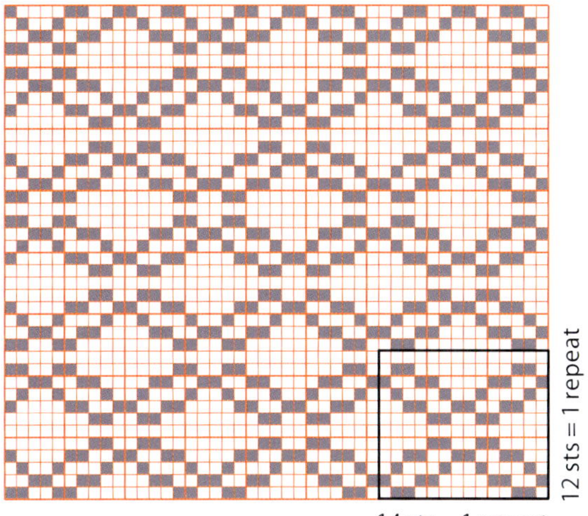

124 Photo > *Page 49*

DMC Embroidery Floss ■311

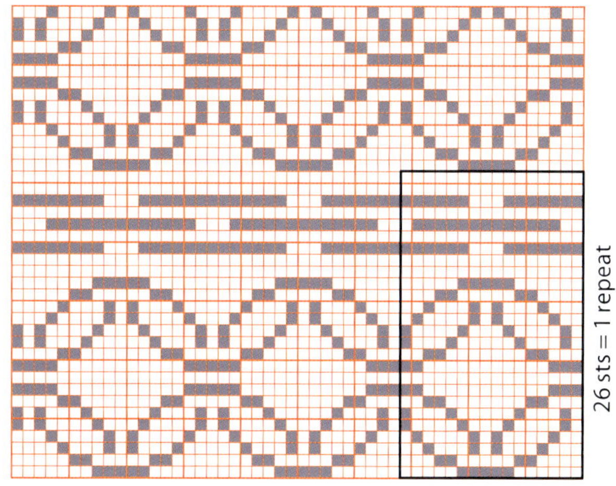

125 Photo > *Page 49*

DMC Embroidery Floss ■311

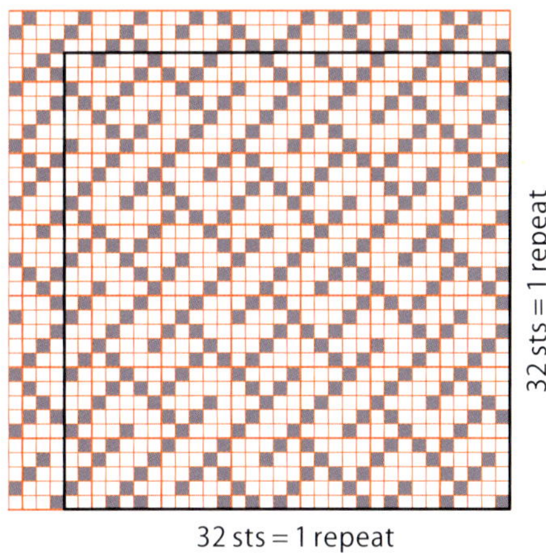

126 Photo > *Page 49*

DMC Embroidery Floss ■311

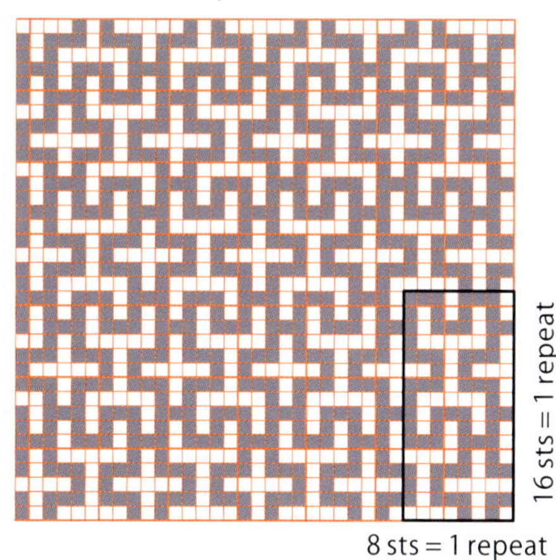

127 Photo > *Page 49*

DMC Embroidery Floss ■311

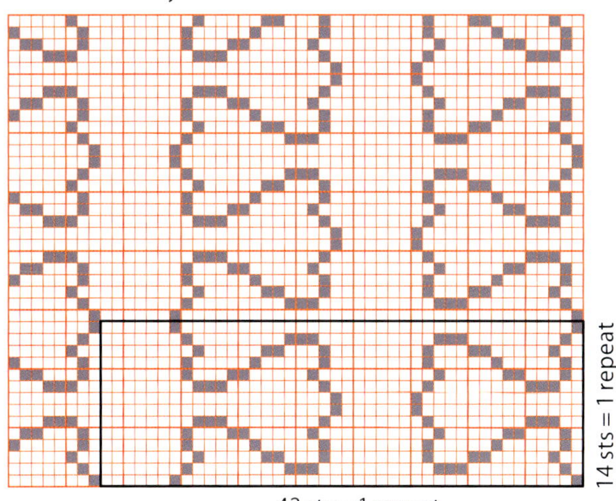

128 Photo > *Page 49*

DMC Embroidery Floss ■311

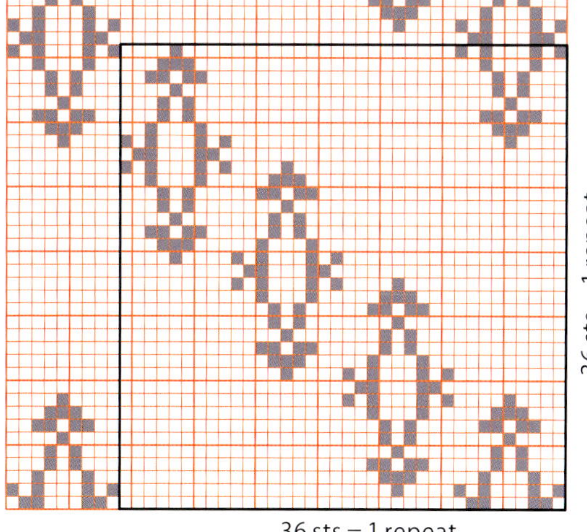

PART FOUR

Flora & Fauna Patterns

These colourful plant and animal motifs feature a variety of leaves, blooms and adorable creatures. Some of the patterns are continuous repeats, while others are standalone statement-making designs.

130 Instructions > page 72

129 Instructions > page 72

131 Instructions > page 72

132 Instructions > page 72

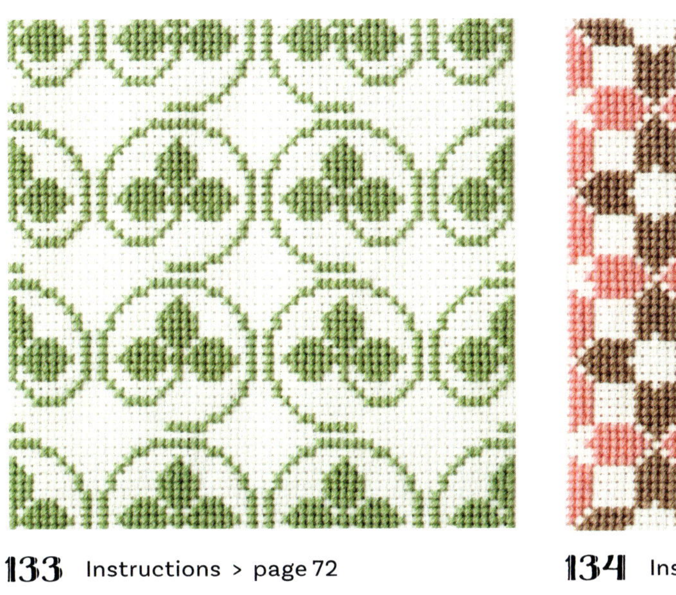

133 Instructions > page 72

134 Instructions > page 72

135 Instructions > page 73

136 Instructions > page 73

137 Instructions > page 73

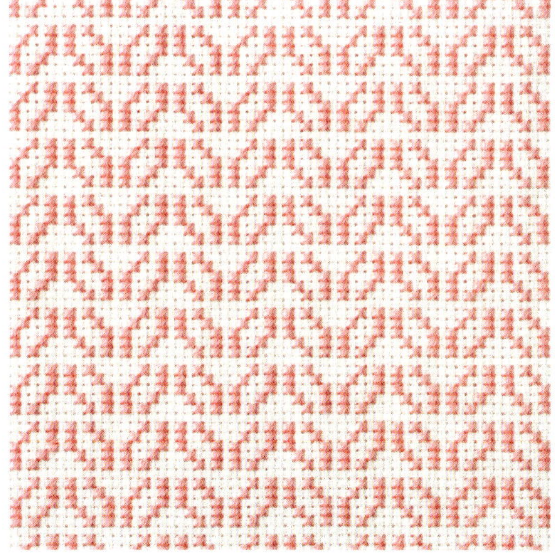

138 Instructions > page 73

Experimenting with Placement

Play with the layout or orientation of a single motif to create unique patterns full of movement. In the following examples, we'll experiment with placement for two floral motifs.

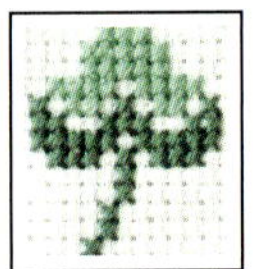

Example Motif

132 Shown on page 60

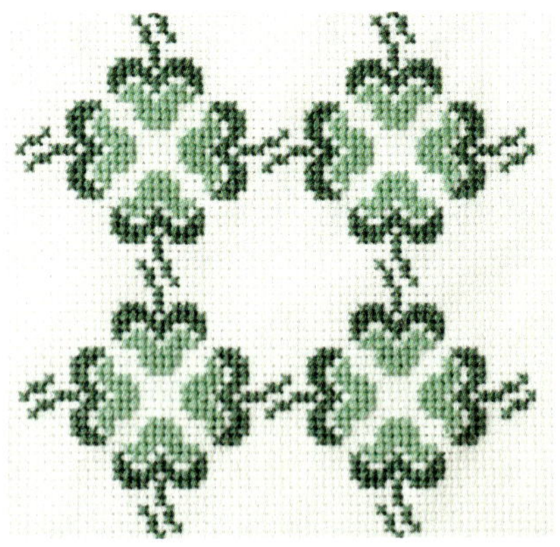

139

Rotate the Motifs

Each trefoil is rotated inward to form a larger circular design. This larger design is then arranged in rows and columns.

DMC Embroidery Floss ■ 3815 ■ 563

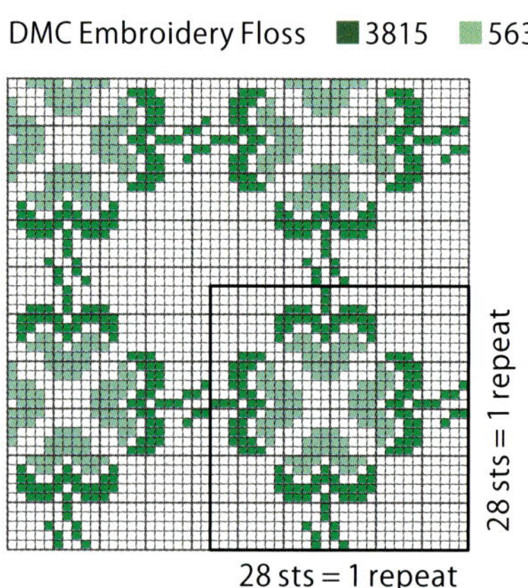

140

Reflect Horizontally

This design is created by flipping the image from left to right as if it was reflected by a mirror. The orientation is changed every other row.

DMC Embroidery Floss ■ 3815 ■ 563

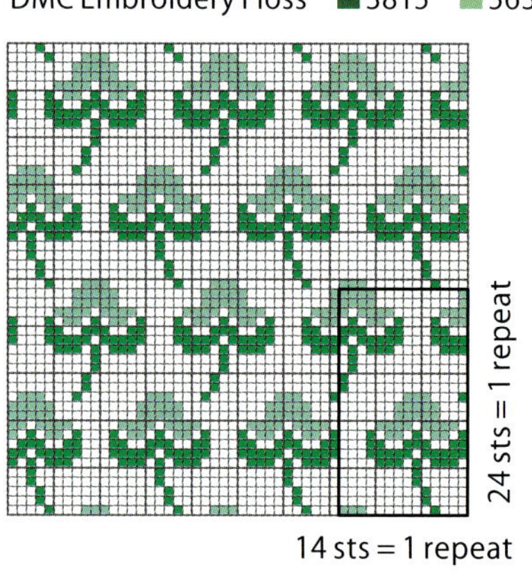

141

Reflect Vertically

Motifs are flipped upside down to create reflecting pairs. The pairs are arranged in a row, and alternating rows are staggered.

DMC Embroidery Floss ■ 3815 ■ 563

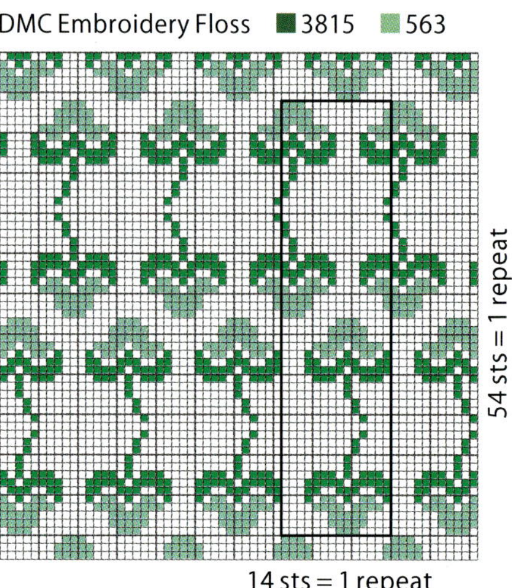

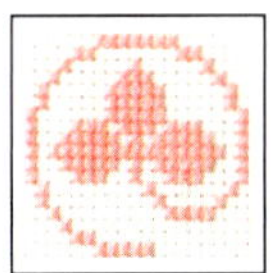

Example Motif

133 Shown on page 61

142

Shift a Motif

One motif has been shifted to create a staggered effect.

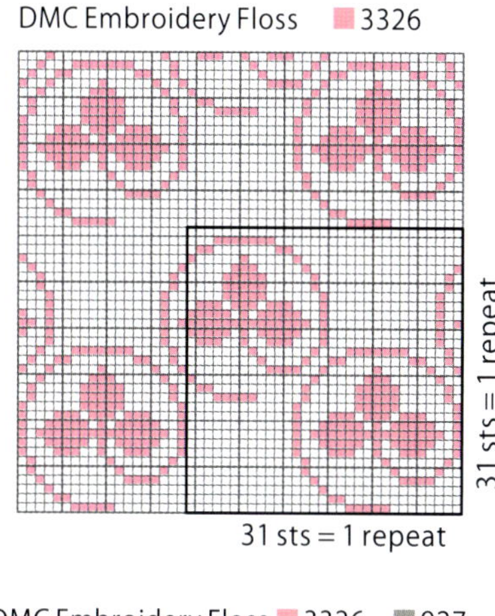

143

Rotate 180°

Motifs are aligned in alternating directions for each column and staggered to create more movement.

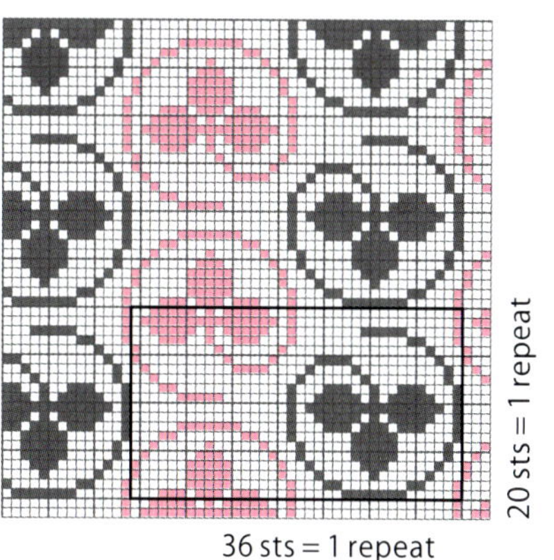

144

Diagonal Rows

Here, the motifs are arranged in diagonal rows that feature mirror images. This may look like the same pattern, but the repeat is actually 855 stitches due to the way the motifs are arranged diagonally.

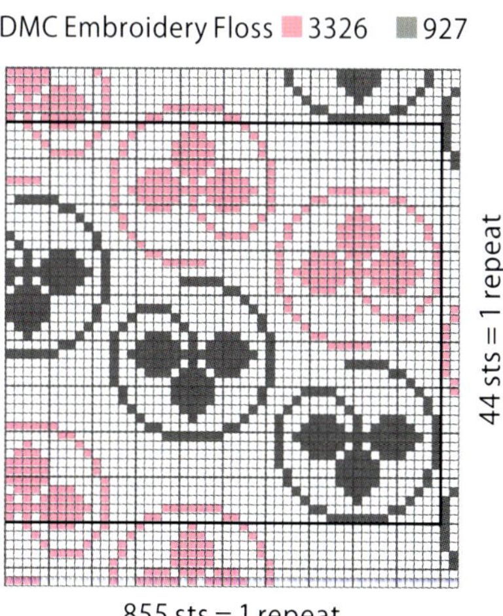

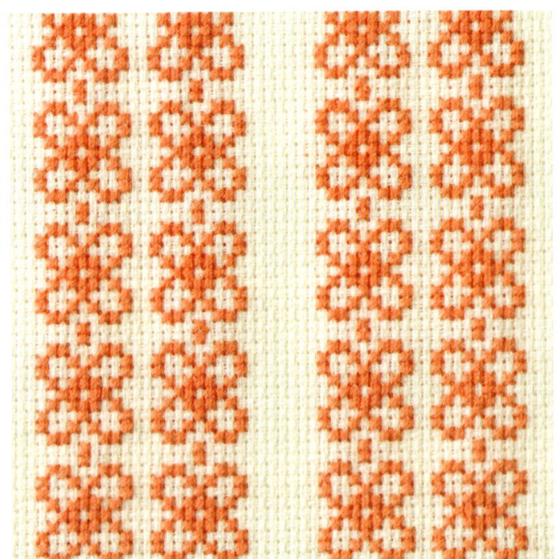

145 Instructions > page 73

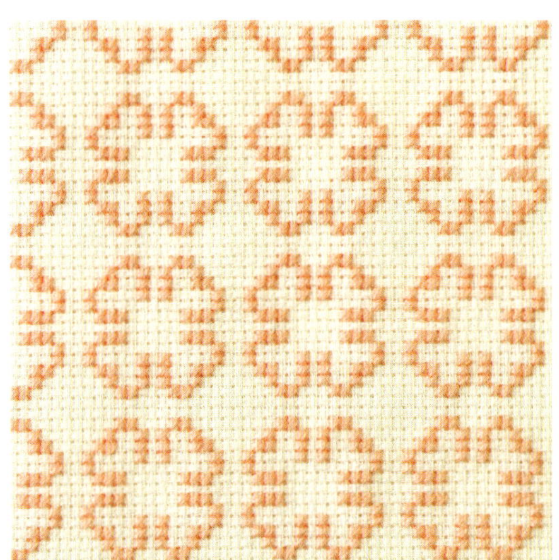

146 Instructions > page 73

147 Instructions > page 74

148 Instructions > page 74

149 Instructions > page 74

150 Instructions > page 74

151 Instructions > page 74

152 Instructions > page 74

153 Instructions > page 75

154 Instructions > page 75

155 Instructions > page 75

156 Instructions > page 76

157 Instructions > page 76

158 Instructions > page 77

159 Instructions > page 78

160 Instructions > page 77

161 Instructions > page 79

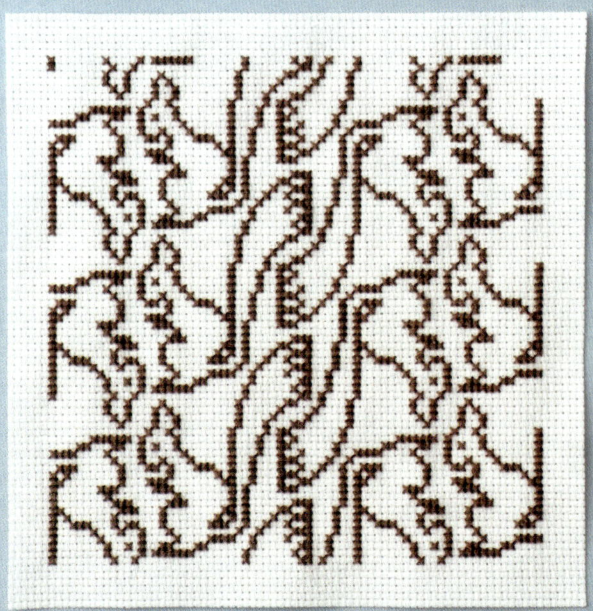

162 Instructions > page 79

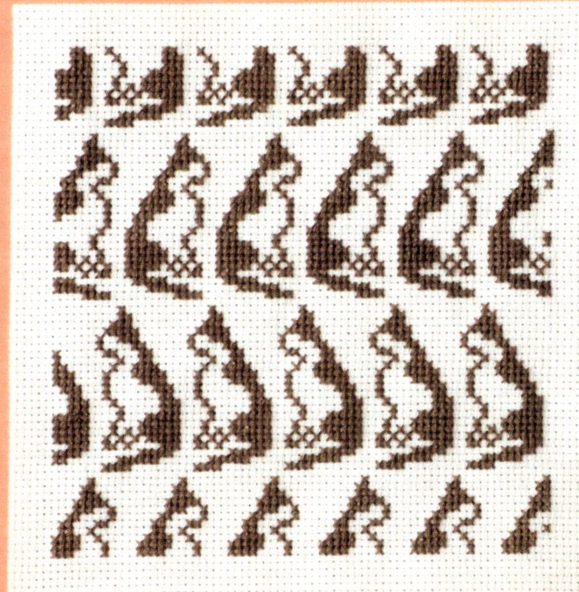

163 Instructions > page 79

164 Instructions > page 79

129 **Photo** > *Page 60*

DMC Embroidery Floss ■ 3354

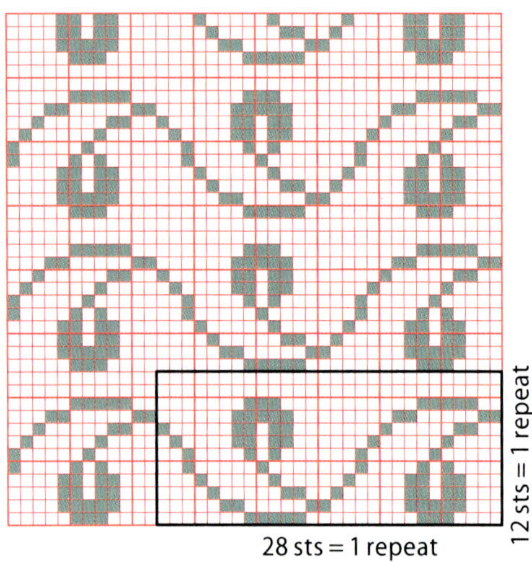

12 sts = 1 repeat

28 sts = 1 repeat

131 **Photo** > *Page 60*

DMC Embroidery Floss ■ 3354

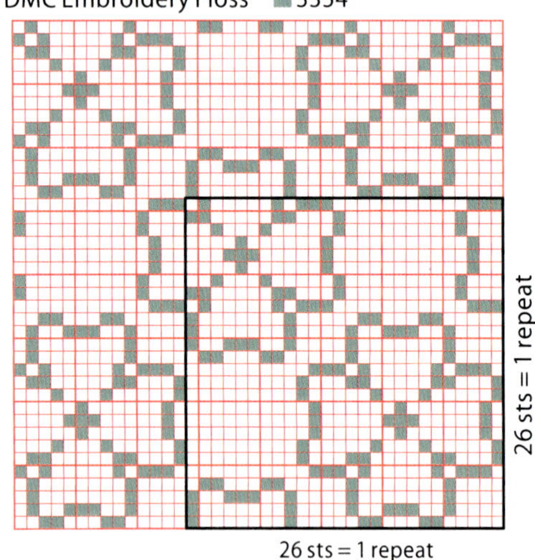

26 sts = 1 repeat

26 sts = 1 repeat

133 **Photo** > *Page 61*

DMC Embroidery Floss ■ 368

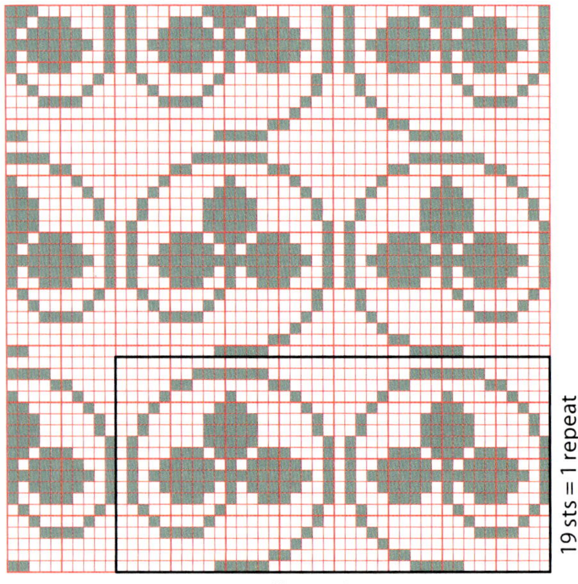

19 sts = 1 repeat

40 sts = 1 repeat

130 **Photo** > *Page 60*

DMC Embroidery Floss ■ 367

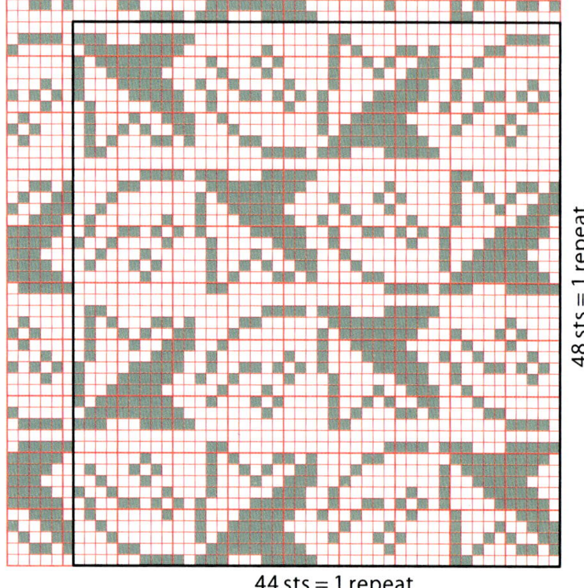

48 sts = 1 repeat

44 sts = 1 repeat

132 **Photo** > *Page 60*

DMC Embroidery Floss ■ 367

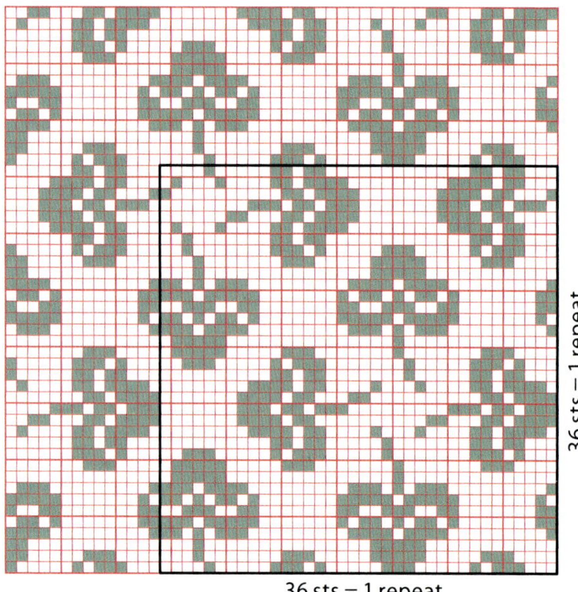

36 sts = 1 repeat

36 sts = 1 repeat

134 **Photo** > *Page 61*

DMC Embroidery Floss ■ 07 ■ 3354

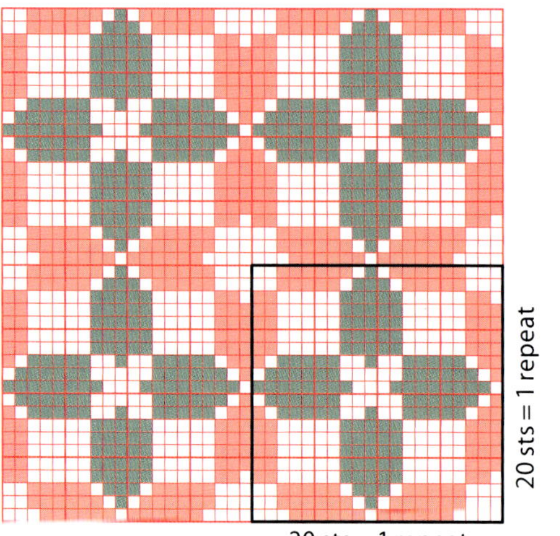

20 sts = 1 repeat

20 sts = 1 repeat

135 Photo > *Page 61*

DMC Embroidery Floss ■ 3354

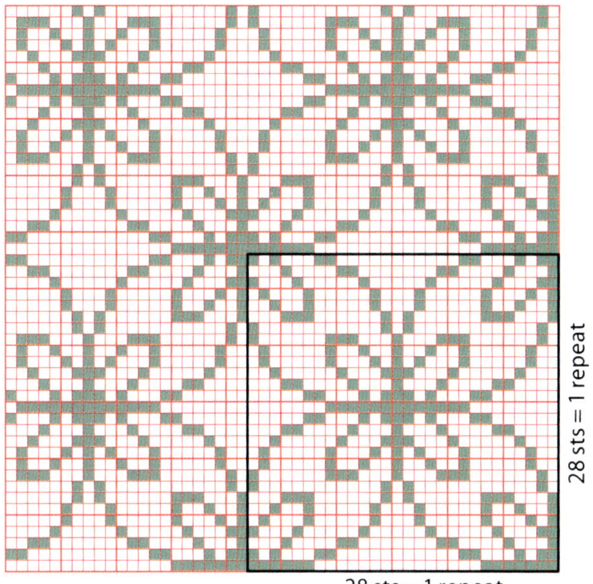

136 Photo > *Page 61*

DMC Embroidery Floss ■ 07 ■ 368

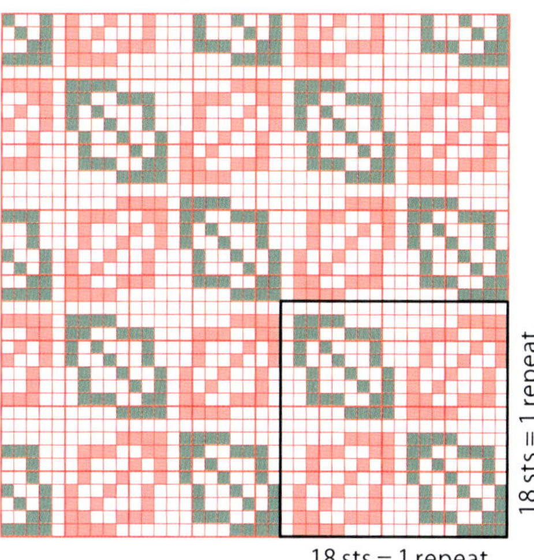

137 Photo > *Page 61*

DMC Embroidery Floss ■ 368

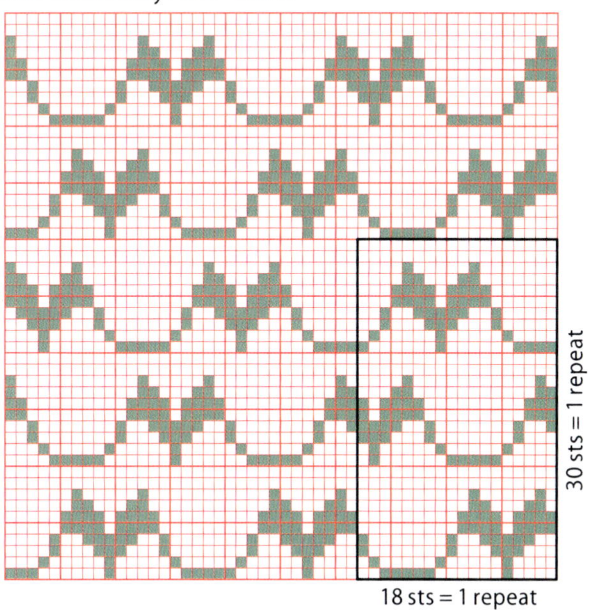

138 Photo > *Page 61*

DMC Embroidery Floss ■ 3354

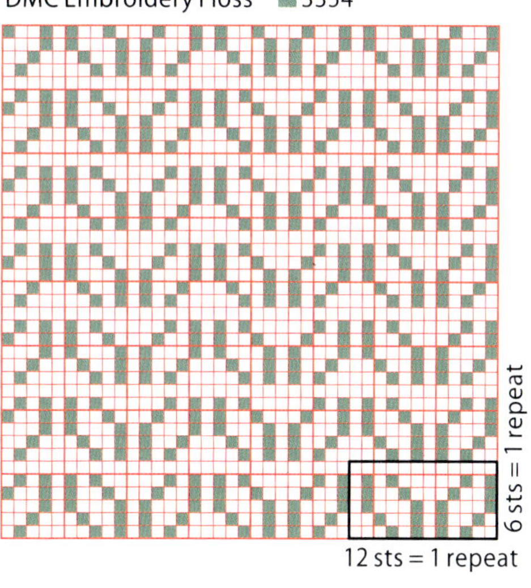

145 Photo > *Page 64*

DMC Embroidery Floss ■ 352

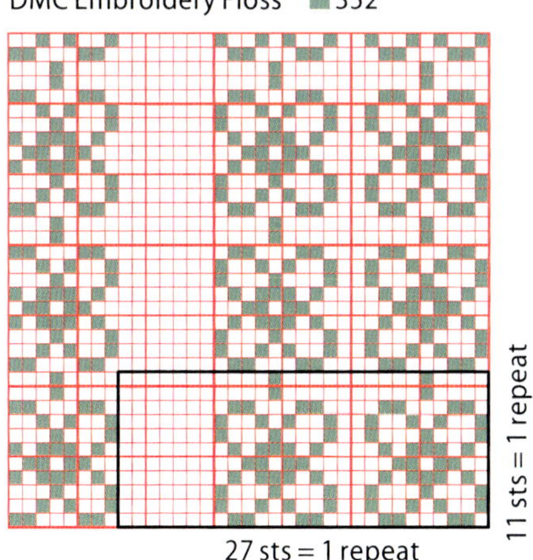

146 Photo > *Page 64*

DMC Embroidery Floss ■ 3779

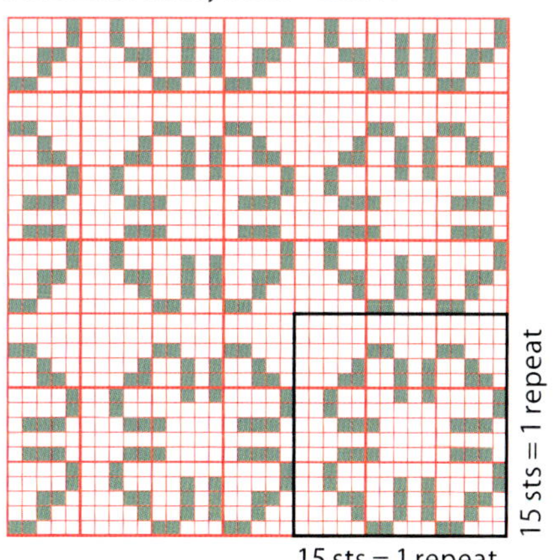

147 Photo > *Page 64*

DMC Embroidery Floss ▪3716

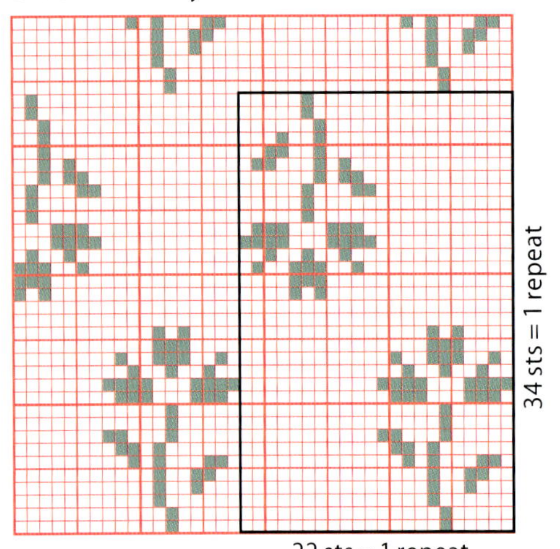

22 sts = 1 repeat

148 Photo > *Page 64*

DMC Embroidery Floss ▪760

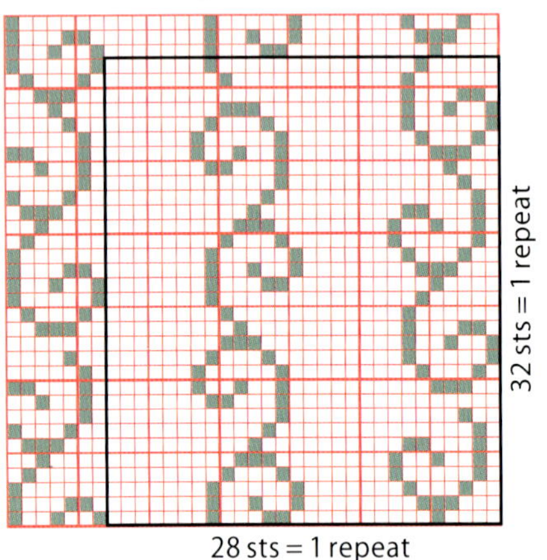

28 sts = 1 repeat

*When continuing on the left side, shift the first repeat up 5 rows.

149-151 Photo > *Page 65*

DMC Embroidery Floss

149	▪3705	▪906	▪12
150	▪3755	▪312	▪322
151	▪3861	▪779	▪3860

31 sts = 1 repeat

152 Photo > *Page 66*

DMC Embroidery Floss ▪3743 Straight stitch (2 strands) ▪3837

153 **Photo** > *Page 66*
DMC Embroidery Floss ■ 792

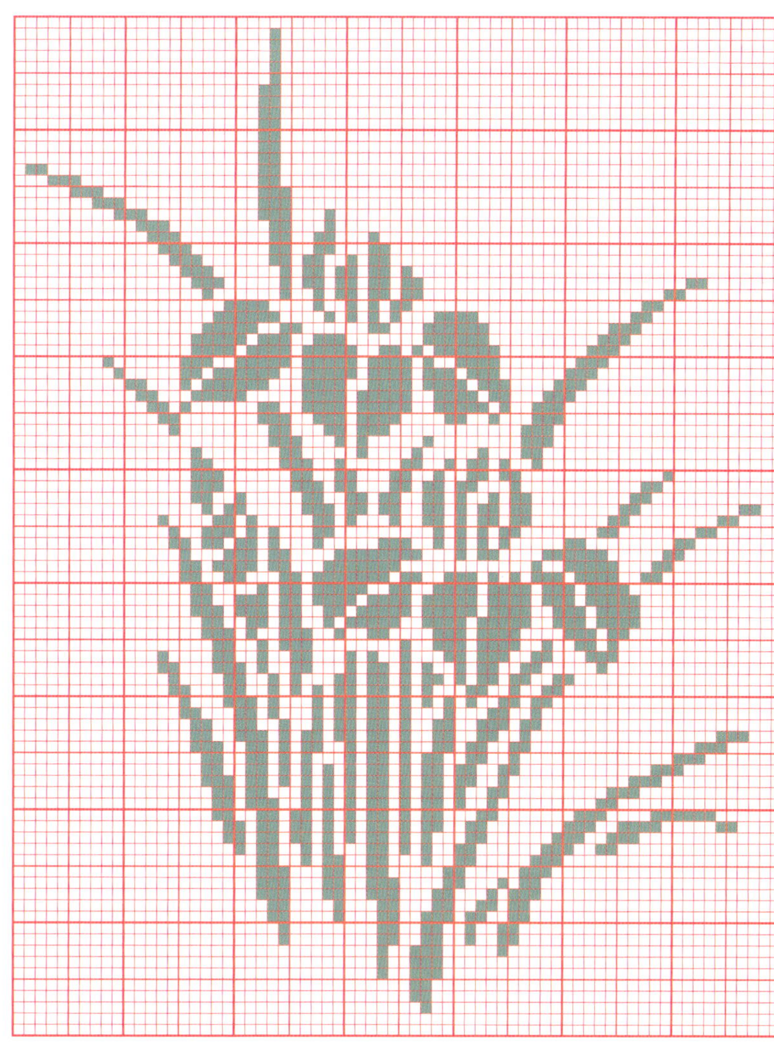

154 **Photo** > *Page 67*
DMC Embroidery Floss ■ 3746

155 **Photo** > *Page 67*
DMC Embroidery Floss ■ 605

156 Photo > *Page 68*

DMC Embroidery Floss ■ 307 ■ 3889

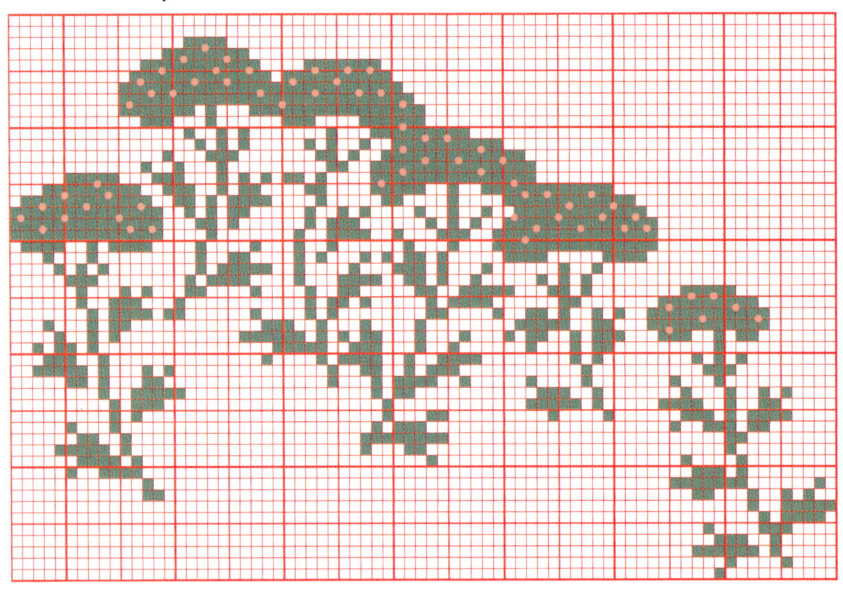

157 Photo > *Page 68*

DMC Embroidery Floss ■ 973

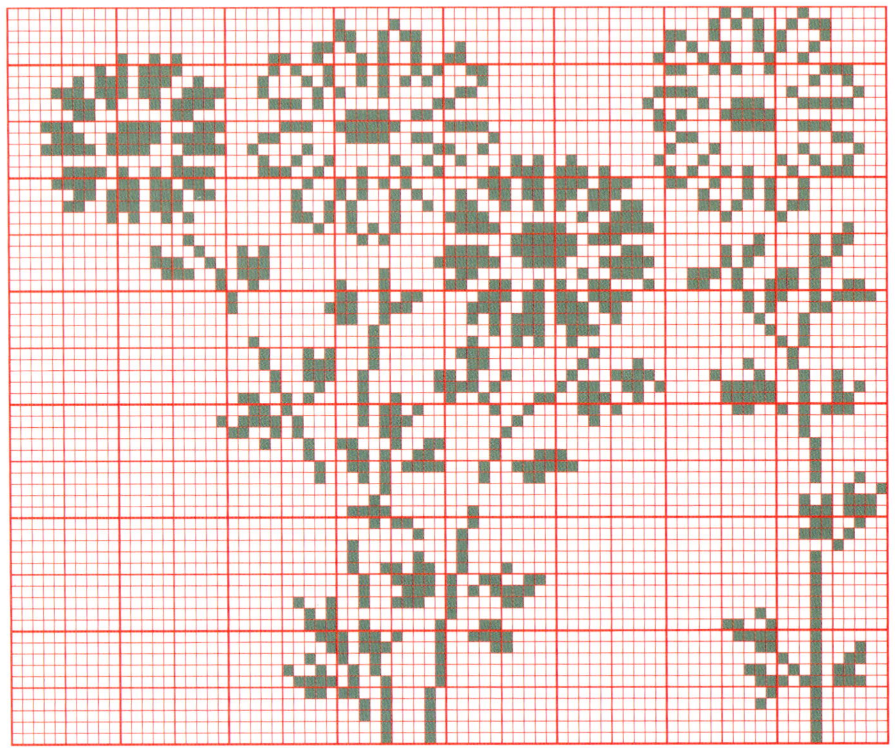

158 **Photo** > *Page 68*
DMC Embroidery Floss ■444

160 **Photo** > *Page 69*
DMC Embroidery Floss ■3607

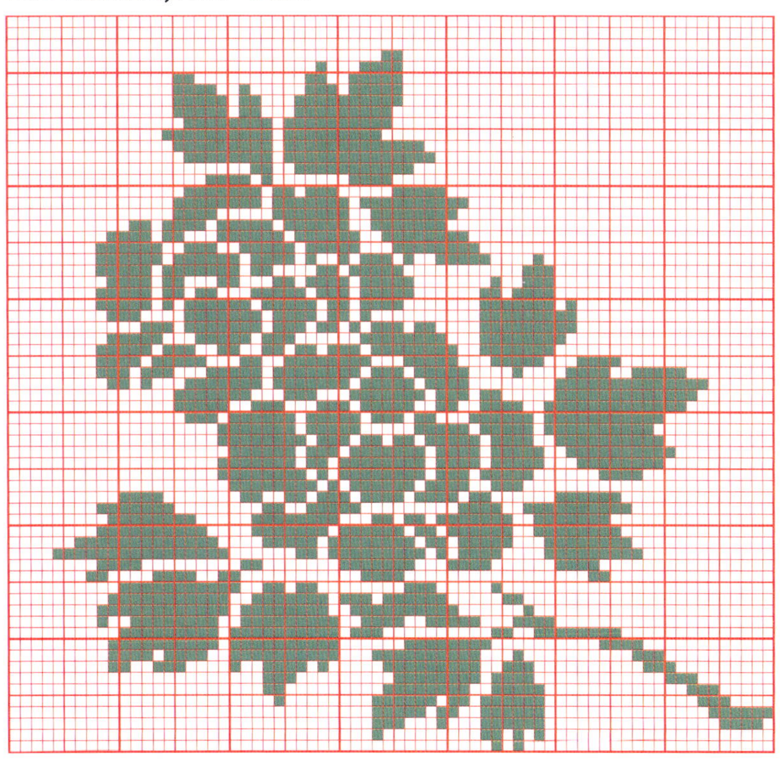

159 **Photo** > *Page 69*

DMC Embroidery Floss ■ 601 (2 skeins)

161 **Photo** > *Page 70*

DMC Embroidery Floss ■ 3810

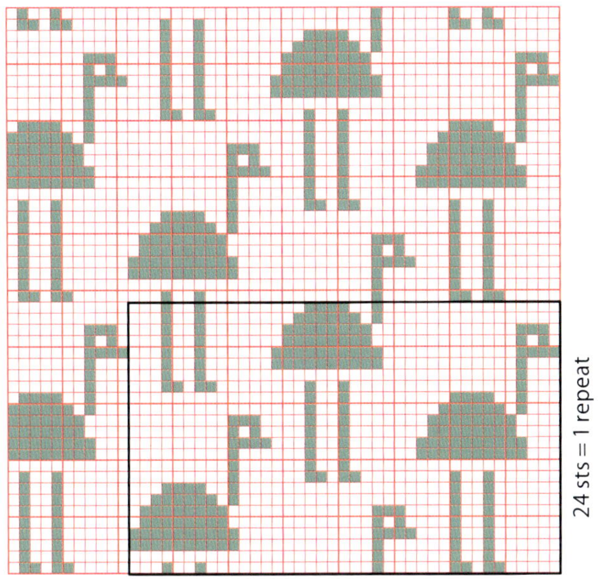

162 **Photo** > *Page 70*

DMC Embroidery Floss ■ 08

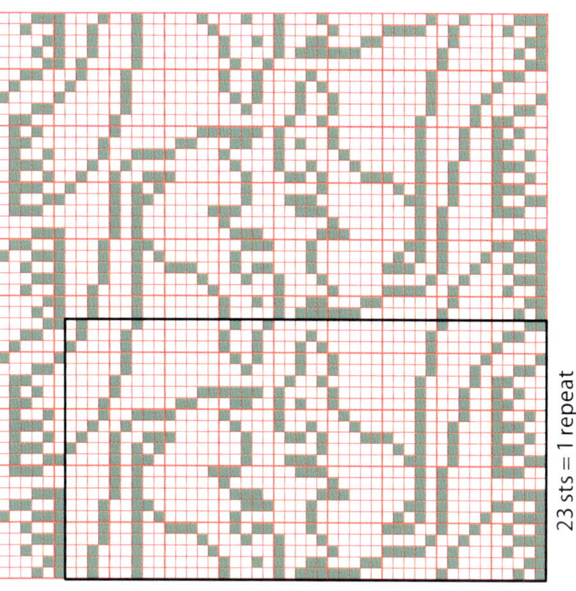

163 **Photo** > *Page 71*

DMC Embroidery Floss ■ 08

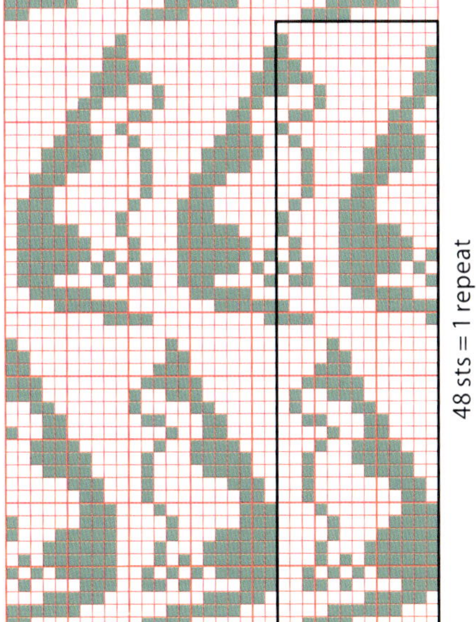

164 **Photo** > *Page 71*

DMC Embroidery Floss ■ 3354 (2 skeins)

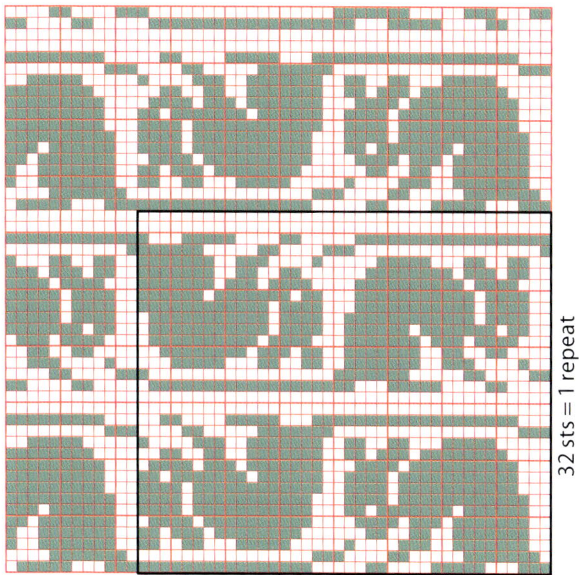

PART FIVE

Borders & Pictorial Motifs

This collection features versatile designs that can be used for a variety of applications. The border motifs are linear and make lovely edging, while the pictorial motifs would be perfect for a main design. You'll also find large-scale motifs that make wonderful tapestries.

165

166

167

Instructions > page 94

Instructions > page 94

Instructions > page 94

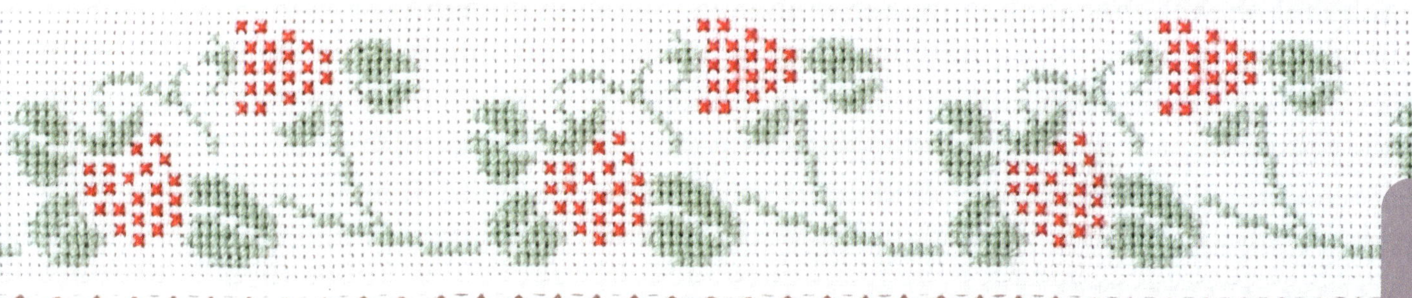

Instructions > page 94

Instructions > page 94

168

169

170

Instructions > page 95

171

Instructions > page 95

172

Instructions > page 95

173

Instructions > page 96

174 Instructions > page 97

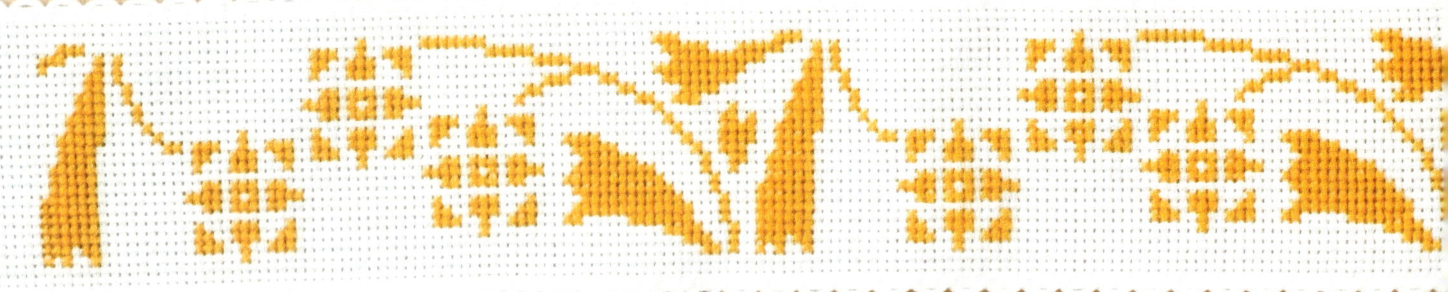

175 Instructions > page 97

176 Instructions > page 97

177 Instructions > page 98

178 Instructions > page 99

179 Instructions > page 100

180 Instructions > page 101

181 Instructions > page 102

182 Instructions > page 102

183 Instructions > page 103

184 Instructions > page 103

Experimenting with Repeats

In this exercise, we'll take a single motif and use it to create continuous patterns. Depending on how you arrange the repeats, you can create a completely unique pattern. The following examples use a simple butterfly motif, but you can apply the same techniques to other motifs.

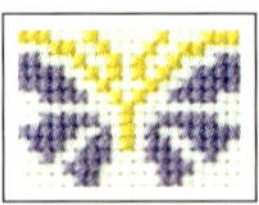

Example Motif

185

Align in Rows and Columns

This design features the butterfly aligned in both horizontal rows and vertical columns.

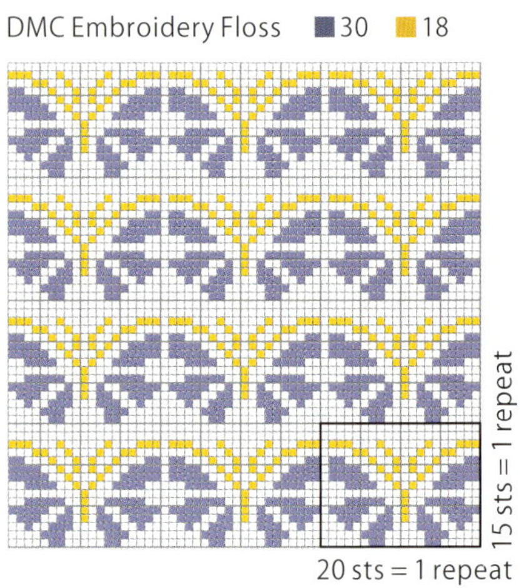

186

Offset the Motif

In this variation, the columns are spaced slightly farther apart and the rows are offset by half a motif.

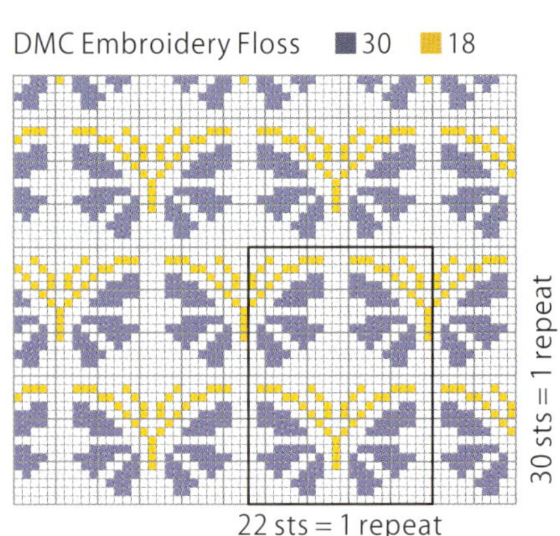

187

Mirror Image

In this example, both the horizontal rows and vertical columns are aligned, but every other row features the mirror image of the motif.

188

Mirror Image + Offset the Motif

Here, two rows of butterflies are positioned to create a mirror image, and then the next two rows are offset by half a motif.

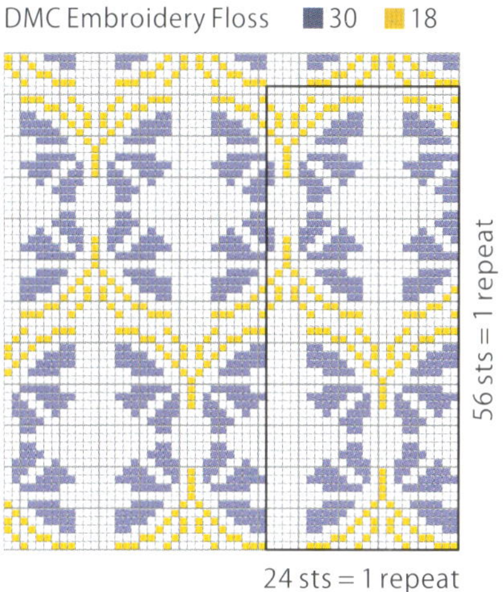

189

Rotate

Each butterfly is rotated 90° and arranged in a circle of four. This creates a checkerboard-like pattern.

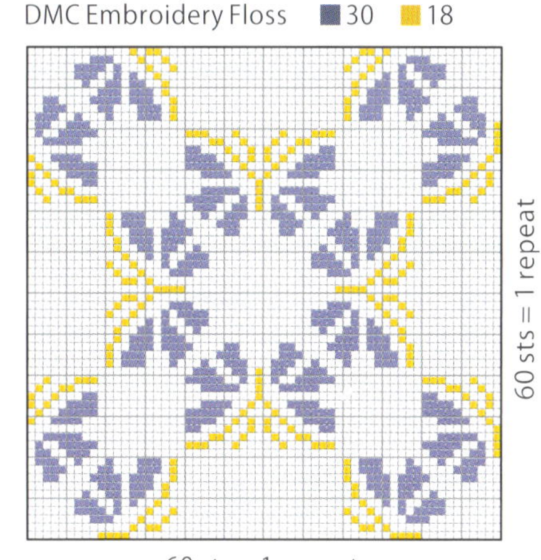

190 Instructions > page 104

191 Instructions > page 105

192 Instructions > page 106

193 Instructions > page 107

194 Instructions > page 107

195 Instructions > page 108

196 Instructions > page 108

197 Instructions > page 109

198 Instructions > page 110

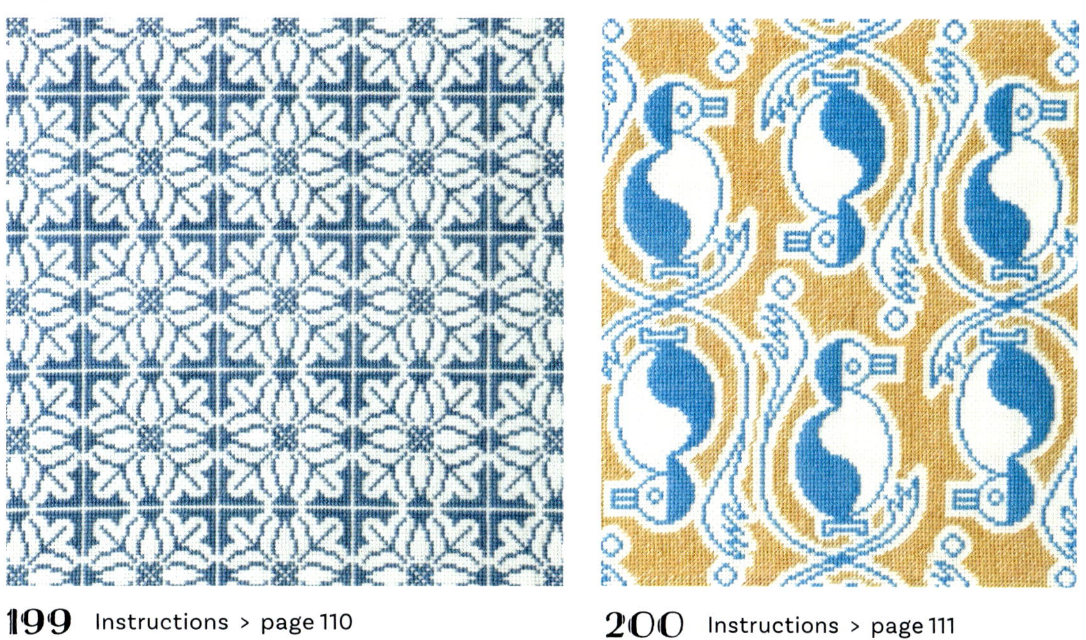

199 Instructions > page 110

200 Instructions > page 111

165 Photo > *Page 80*

DMC Embroidery Floss ■413

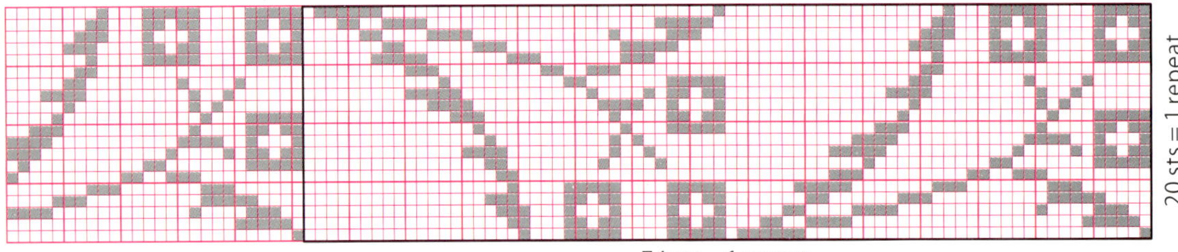

166 Photo > *Page 80*

DMC Embroidery Floss ■3813 ■309

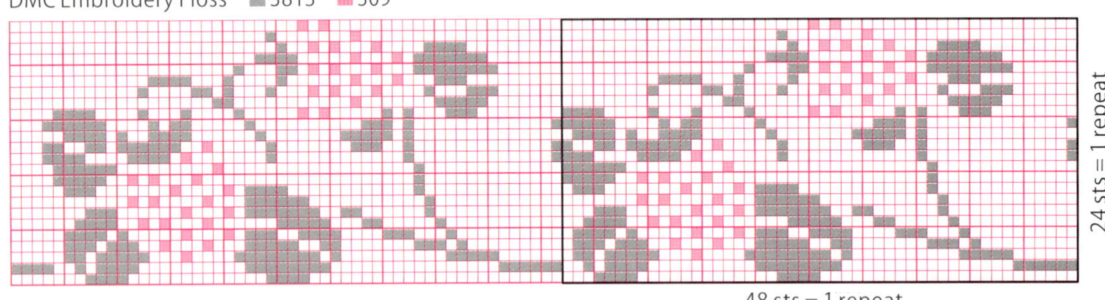

167 Photo > *Page 80*

DMC Embroidery Floss ■309

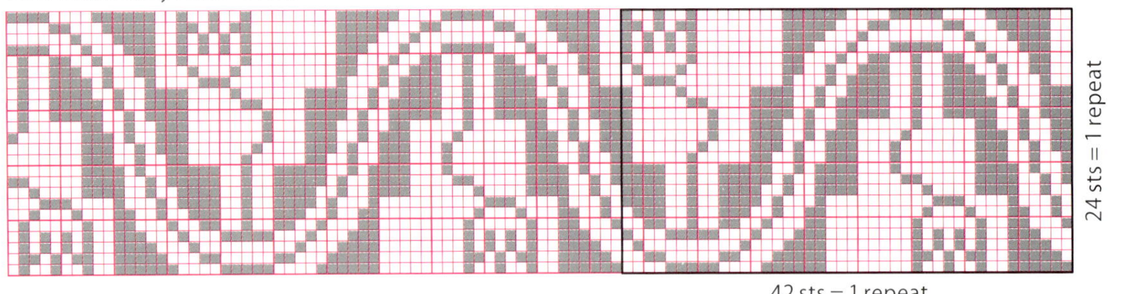

168 Photo > *Page 81*

DMC Embroidery Floss ■413 ■309

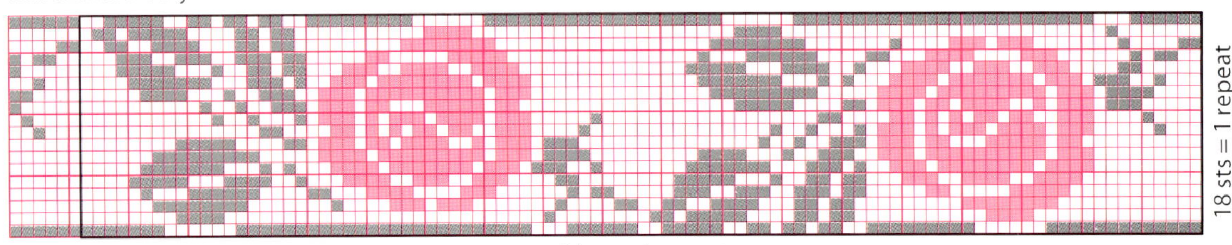

169 Photo > *Page 81*

DMC Embroidery Floss ■3813

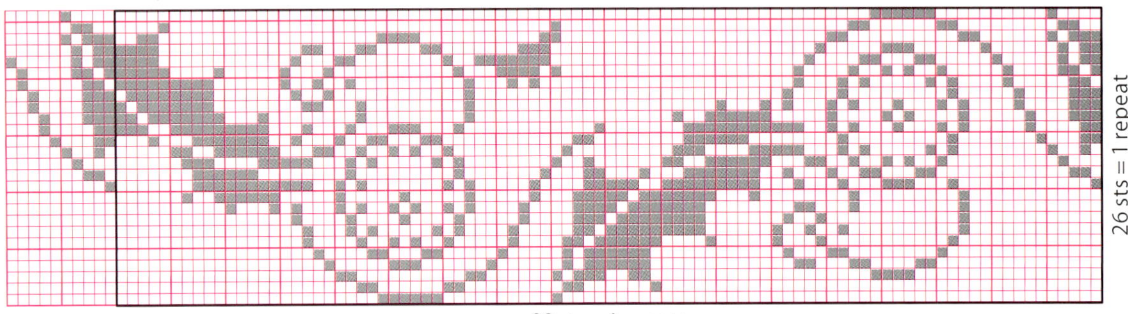

170 Photo > Page 82
DMC Embroidery Floss
987 742
54 sts = 1 repeat
26 sts = 1 repeat
171 Photo > Page 82
DMC Embroidery Floss
318
52 sts = 1 repeat
14 sts = 1 repeat
172 Photo > Page 82
DMC Embroidery Floss
987 (| = Backstitch with 2 strands)
51 sts = 1 repeat
24 sts = 1 repeat

173 Photo > *Page 83*

DMC Embroidery Floss ■318 ■742

174 Photo > *Page 84*

DMC Embroidery Floss ■3858 ■783 (// = Half cross stitch with 1 strand)

175 Photo > *Page 84*

DMC Embroidery Floss ■783

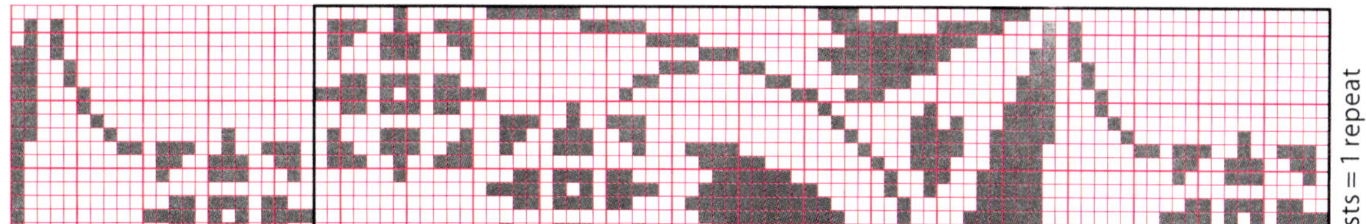

176 Photo > *Page 85*

DMC Embroidery Floss ■3848 ■3858 •3858 French knot (wrap twice)

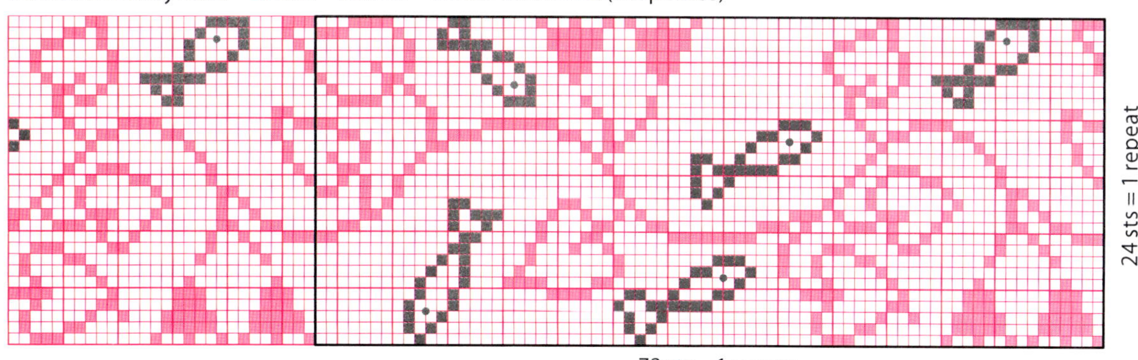

177 **Photo** > *Page 86*

DMC Embroidery Floss ■3808

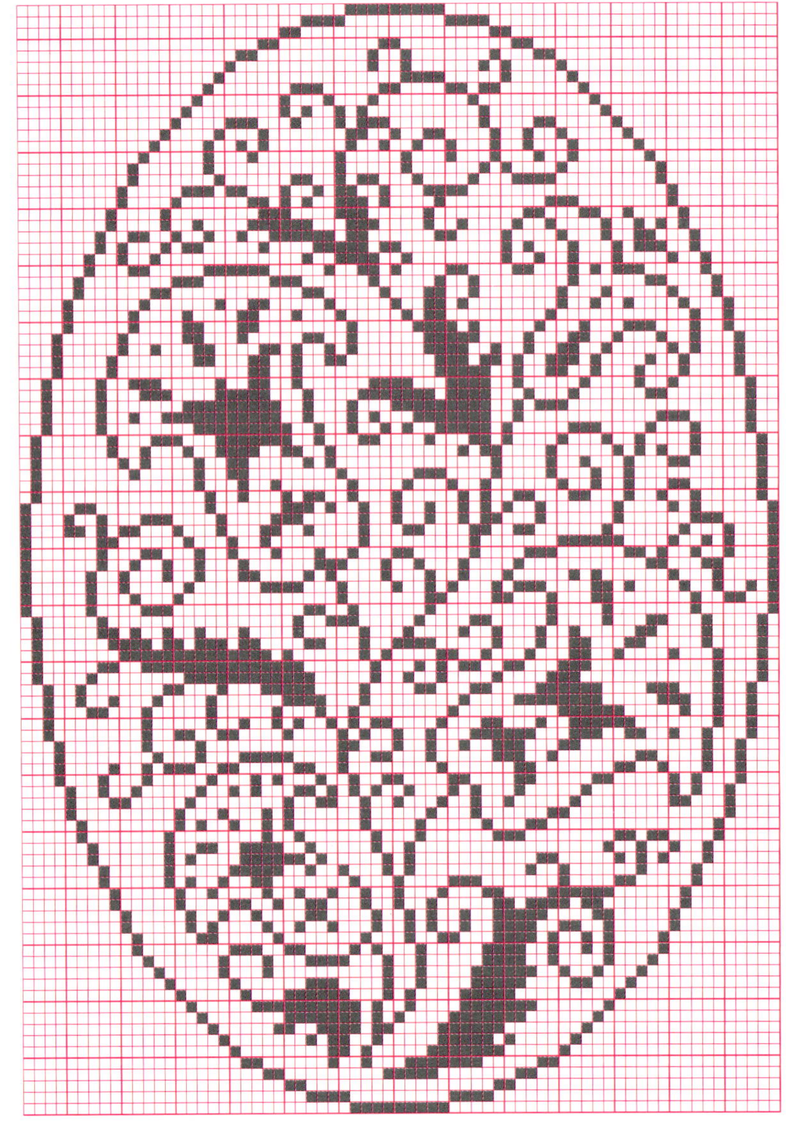

178 Photo > *Page 86*

DMC Embroidery Floss ■31 ■32

179 Photo > *Page 87*

DMC Embroidery Floss ■318 ■921 ■336

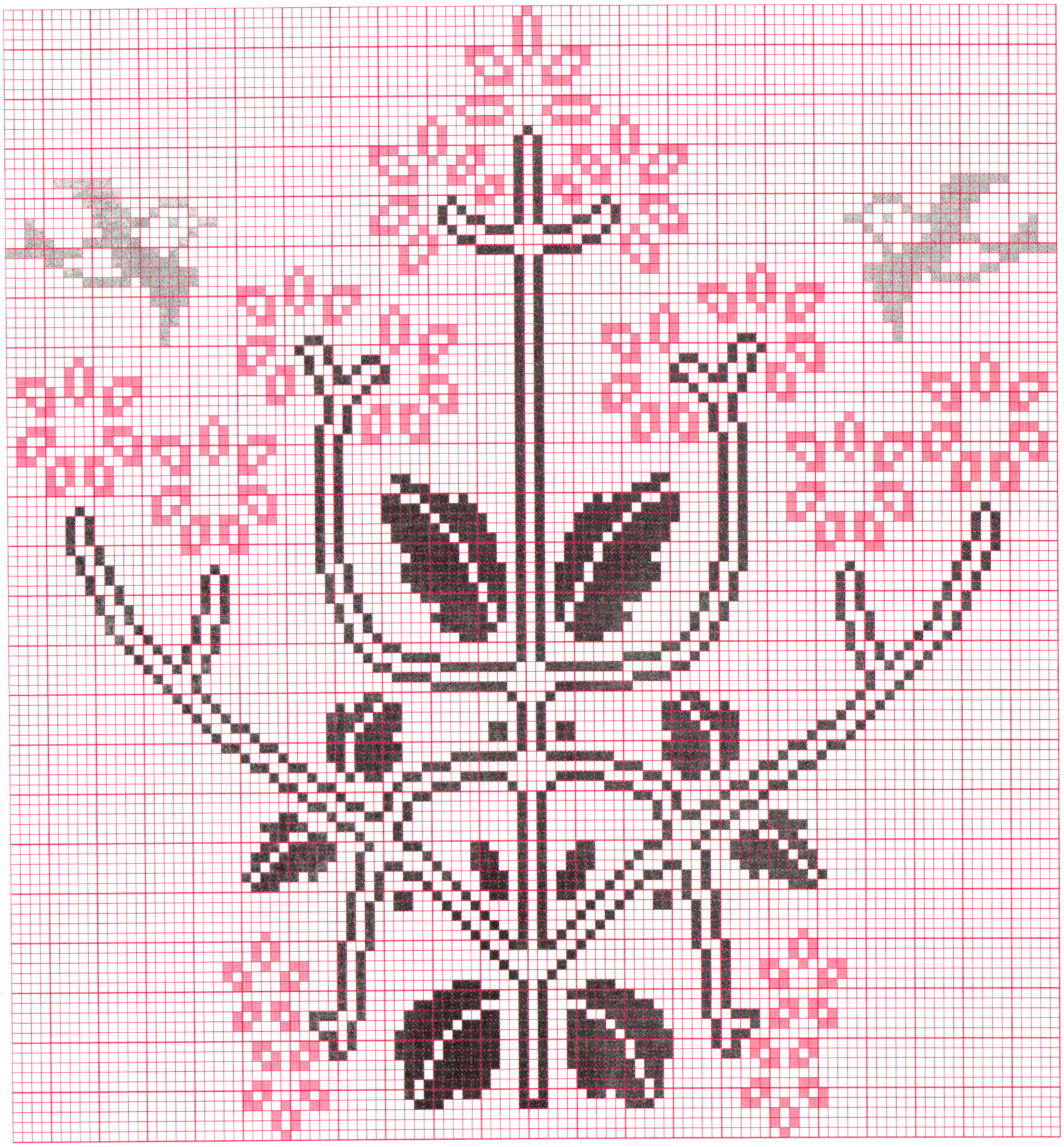

180 **Photo** > *Page 87*

DMC Embroidery Floss ■470 (Leaves) ■826 (Lower birds) ■3755 (Upper birds)

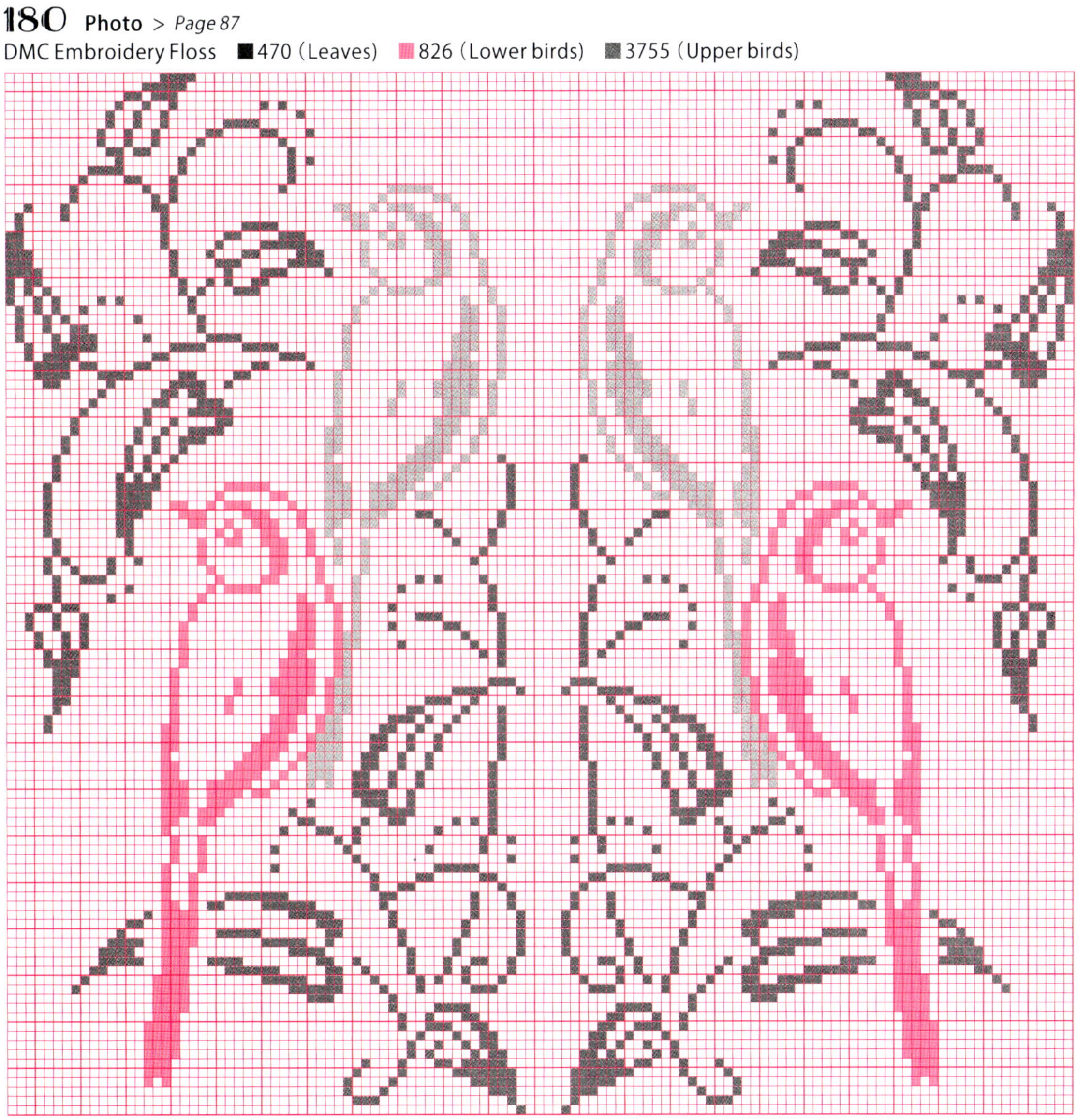

181 **Photo** > *Page 88*

DMC Embroidery Floss ■451 ■335

182 **Photo** > *Page 89*

DMC Embroidery Floss

■3722

183 Photo > *Page 89*
DMC Embroidery Floss ■316

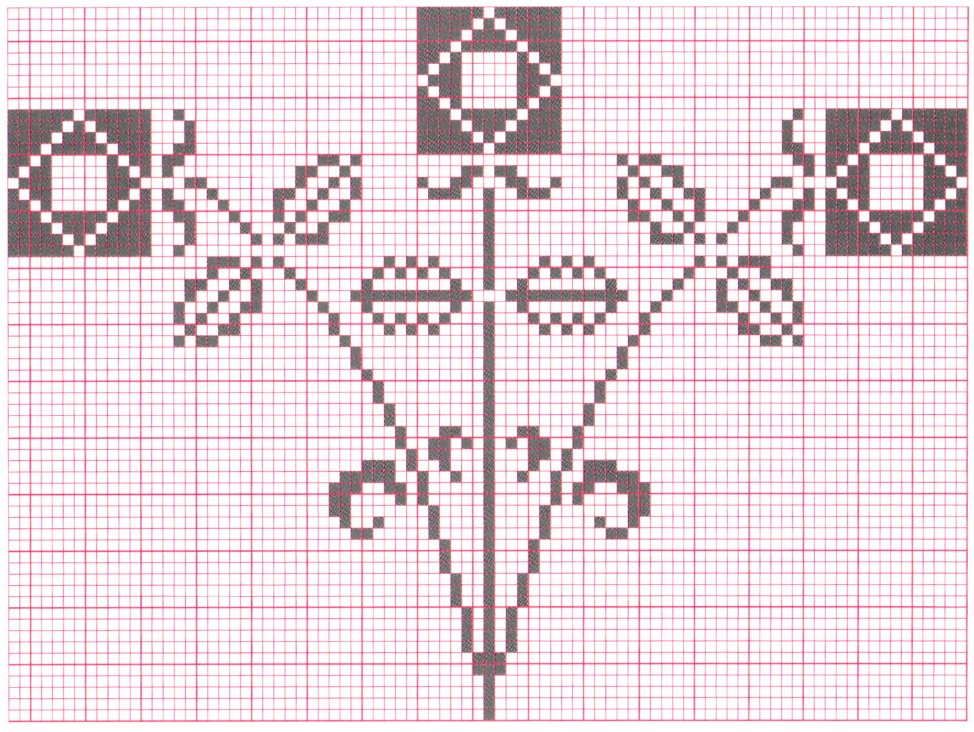

184 Photo > *Page 89*
DMC Embroidery Floss ■208

190 **Photo** > *Page 92*

DMC Embroidery Floss ■ 326 (4 skeins)

191 **Photo** > *Page 92*

DMC Embroidery Floss ■ 3814 (4 skeins)

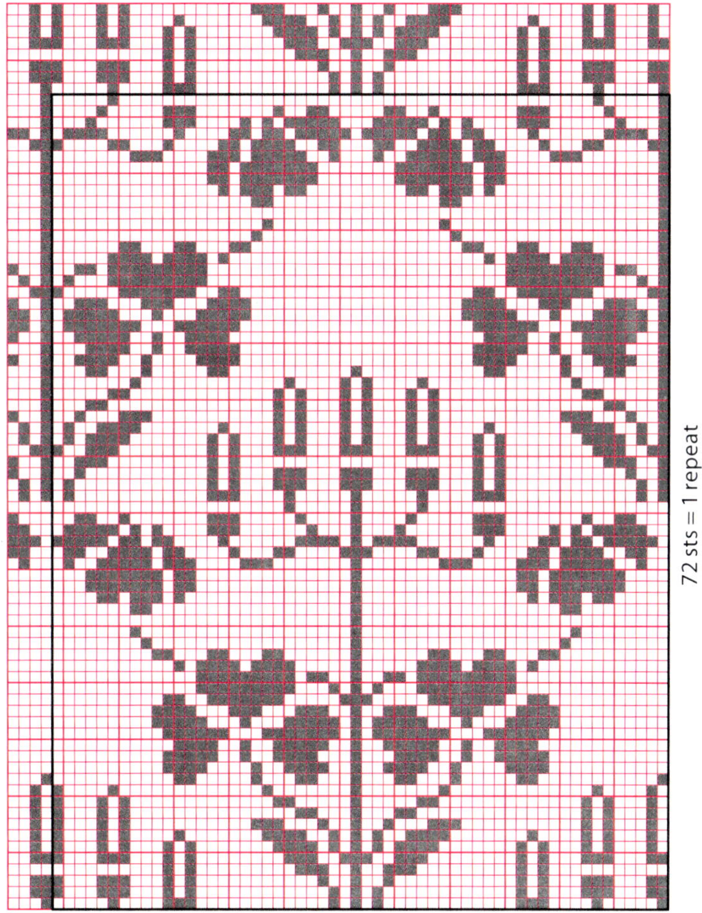

192 Photo > *Page 92*

DMC Embroidery Floss ■648 (2 skeins) ■563 (1 skein)

193 Photo > *Page 92*

DMC Embroidery Floss ■563 (2 skeins) ■3687 (2 skeins)

194 Photo > *Page 92*

DMC Embroidery Floss

■318 (1skein)

■326 (1skein)

195 **Photo** > *Page 92*

DMC Embroidery Floss ■3849 (2 skeins)

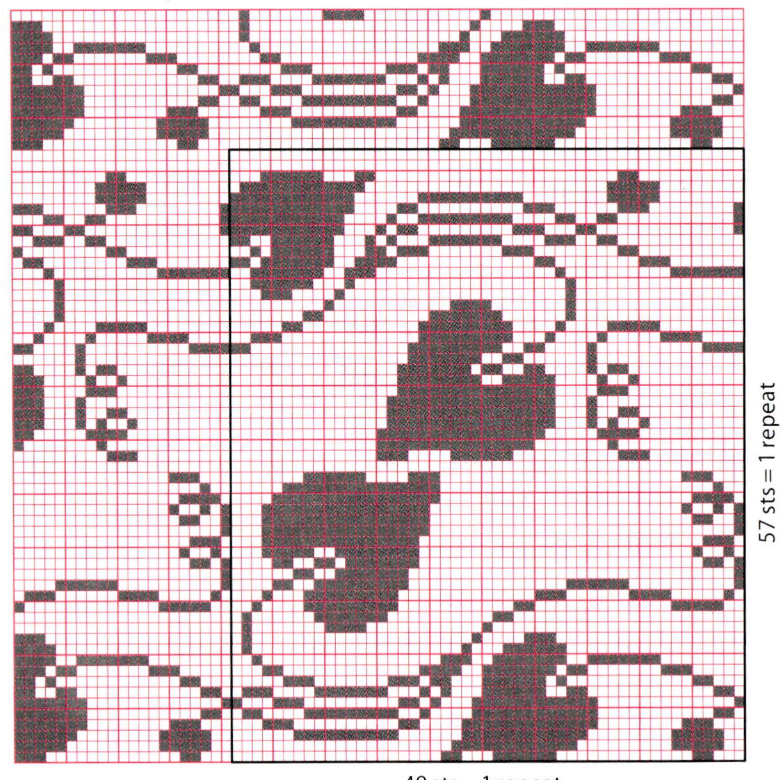

57 sts = 1 repeat

49 sts = 1 repeat

196 **Photo** > *Page 93*

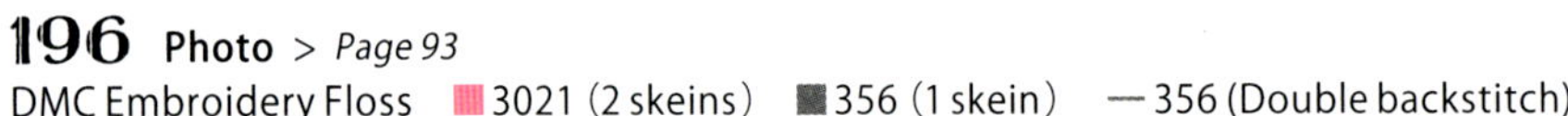

DMC Embroidery Floss ■3021 (2 skeins) ■356 (1 skein) —356 (Double backstitch)

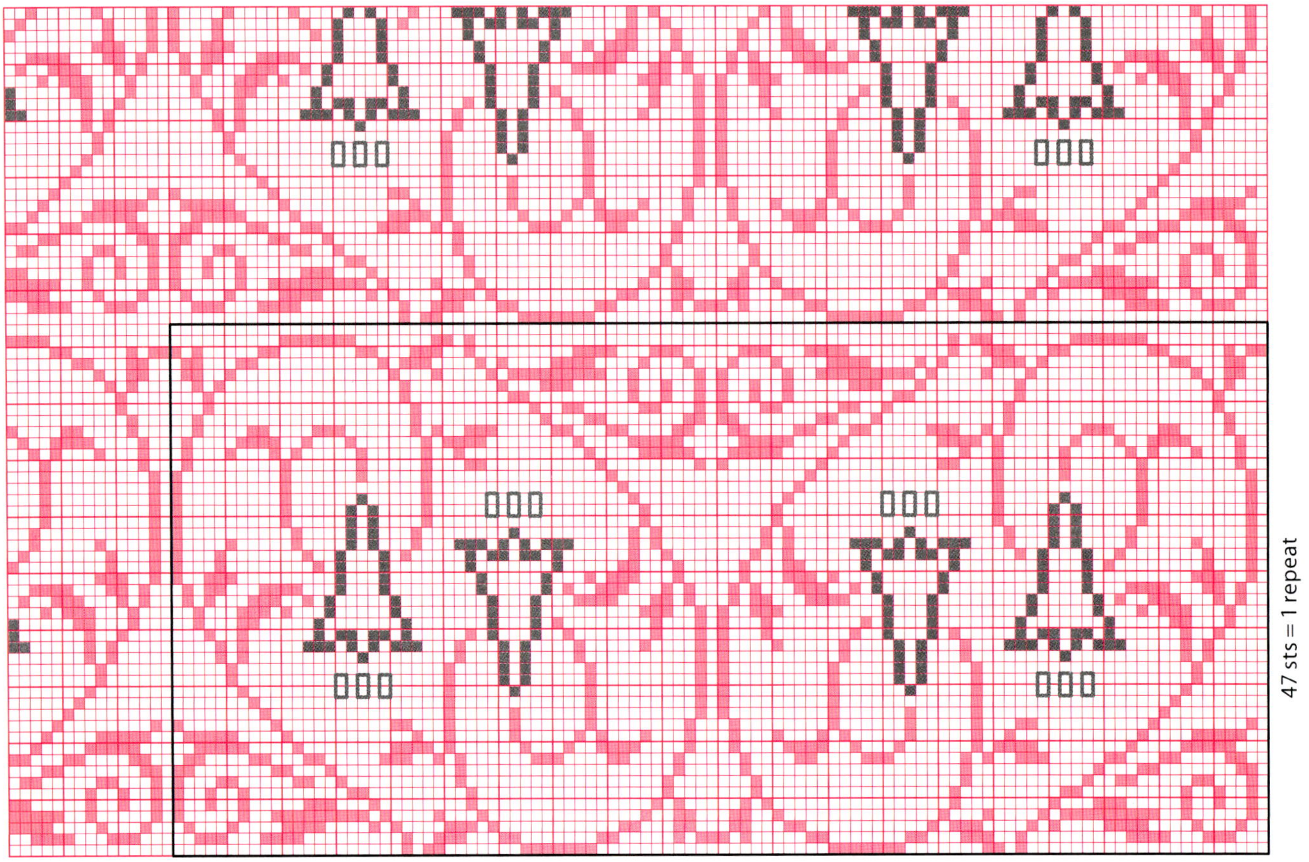

47 sts = 1 repeat

100 sts = 1 repeat

197 **Photo** > *Page 93*

DMC Embroidery Floss ■ 20 (3 skeins) ■ 518 (1 skein)

198 Photo > *Page 93*

DMC Embroidery Floss ■3845 (2 skeins) ■894 (2 skeins)

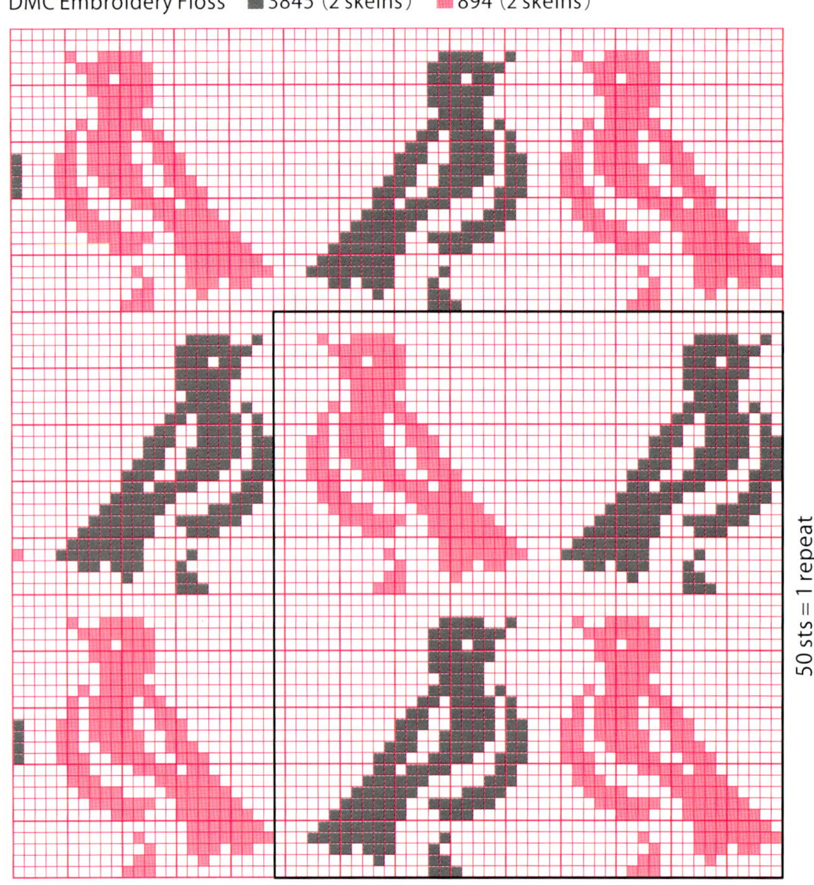

199 Photo > *Page 93*

DMC Embroidery Floss ■518 (4 skeins)

200 Photo > *Page 93*

Photo > Page 93

DMC Embroidery Floss ■3845 (2 skeins) ■612 (1 skein) Half cross stitch (2 strands)

A DAVID AND CHARLES BOOK

David and Charles is an imprint of David and Charles, Ltd
Suite A, Tourism House, Pynes Hill, Exeter, EX2 5WS

Cross stitch de Tanoshimu Wa no Moyo
Cross stitch de Tanoshimu Retoro Moyo
Cross stitch de Tanoshimu Kimono Moyo
Original Japanese edition published by KAWADE SHOBO SHINSHA Ltd Publishers through Timo Associates, Inc., Tokyo. English language rights, translation & production by World Book Media, LLC

Embroidery production: Sihomi Sato
Photography: Rika Wada (mobiile,inc.)

First published in the UK and USA in 2025

A catalogue record for this book is available from the British Library.

ISBN-13: 9781446316047 paperback
ISBN-13: 9781446316269 EPUB

This book has been printed on paper from approved suppliers and made from pulp from sustainable sources.

Printed in China by Mei Tu Ya Graphic Ltd for:
David and Charles, Ltd
Suite A, Tourism House, Pynes Hill, Exeter, EX2 5WS

10 9 8 7 6 5 4 3 2 1